A Concise Dictionary of Confusables

Other dictionaries edited by B. A. Phythian

A Concise Dictionary of Correct English
B. A. Phythian

A Concise Dictionary of English Idioms
William Freeman
Revised by B. A. Phythian

A Concise Dictionary of English Slang and Colloquialisms
B. A. Phythian

A Concise Dictionary of Foreign Expressions
B. A. Phythian

A Concise Dictionary of Confusables

B. A. Phythian

*H*eadway · Hodder & Stoughton

First published 1989

Copyright © B. A. Phythian 1989

British Library Cataloguing in Publication Data

A concise dictionary of confusables
  1. English language. Dictionaries
  I. Phythian, B. A. (Brian Arthur)
  423

  ISBN 0 340 49533 2 Boards
  ISBN 0 340 49534 0 Paperback

Printed and bound in Great Britain for
Hodder and Stoughton Educational,
a division of Hodder and Stoughton Ltd,
Mill Road, Dunton Green, Sevenoaks, Kent,
by Richard Clay Ltd, Bungay, Suffolk

Preface

Many people think that a conventional dictionary defines the correct use of words. Not so: it records how words are currently and generally used, which is far from being the same thing, and compilers refrain from expressing any opinions about 'correctness', though they give guidance about status by categorising certain words as 'slang', 'informal', 'chiefly US' and so on.

The compiler of a handbook of English usage, such as this one, is not restricted to recording how words are used. He is free to say how they ought to be used so as to avoid ambiguity, lack of clarity or plain ugliness. He may criticise sloppy tendencies or insist on the observance of fine but important distinctions between words. Very few English words are interchangeable in all respects, though conventional dictionaries do not have the space to demonstrate how they differ in precise shades of meaning. Yet it is in those very shades that the richness of English resides. Truly correct, precise and idiomatic English is rooted in an understanding of them.

This book defines many hundreds of words, mainly in pairs, that may give rise to confusion for a variety of reasons. Perhaps the words merely look or sound alike; perhaps they are interchangeable in some contexts but not in others; perhaps they are very closely related, or just commonly misunderstood or misused because of public carelessness or ignorance. Whatever the cause of confusion, we hope the study of it will be informative and entertaining.

B.A.P.

Note

Not all the words listed in this dictionary are fully defined. Only areas of definition that may give rise to confusion are dealt with.

Within entries, the use of bold face indicates cross-reference.

A

able, capable   Both mean *having the necessary power,* but *able* has a slightly more active feel. A person who says he is *able* to do a job for you is nearer to doing it than one who says he is *capable* of doing it. See **ability**.

ability, capability, capacity   There is overlap here, but some shades of difference are discernible.

> *ability*:   the power (mental or physical) to do something (*The ability to speak Italian*).
>
> *capablity*:   the quality of being capable or competent, or of being available or inclined to do something; potential; fitness to do something (*The capabilities of a car*).
>
> *capacity*:   the power of containing, absorbing, holding; the ability to produce (*A capacity for hard work*).

One would usually say that a person has the ability, and a machine the capability, to do something, and that a tank has the capacity rather than the ability to hold a certain amount. See **able**.

abjure, adjure   The *-jure* component means *swear.*

> *abjure*:   renounce on oath.
>
> *adjure*:   charge (someone) on oath (to do something); solemnly request.

One may *abjure* alcohol or be *adjured* by someone to abstain from it.

abnormal, subnormal   The prefixes *ab-* and *sub-* mean *away from* and *below* respectively, so that *abnormal* means *different from normal, not normal,* and *subnormal* means *below normal, inferior to normal.* Applied to a person's intelligence, *subnormal* is harsh; *below average* or, as the case may be, *mentally handicapped* is kinder.

abrogate, arrogate   *Abrogate,* meaning *repeal, abolish,* is usually applied to a law, rule or custom. *Arrogate* is usually found in the expression *arrogate to oneself,* meaning *claim for oneself without justification or unreasonably;* the world is related to *arrogant* and has some of its toning.

absence, absenteeism

> *absence*:   state of being away.
>
> *absenteeism*:   persistent absence, especially without good reason.

abstemious, abstinent

> *abstemious*: sparing, especially in the amount one eats or drinks.
> *abstinent*: abstaining, especially from indulgence.

The difference between being *abstemious* and *abstinent* is the difference between moderation and doing without.

See **abstemiousness**.

abstemiousness, abstinence, abstinency, abstention All these have to do with abstaining in one way or another. The difference between *abstemiousness* and *abstinence* is the same as that between **abstemious** and **abstinent**.

> *abstemiousness*: moderation, especially with food or drink.
> *abstinence*: abstaining, especially from indulgence.
> *abstinency*: the habit of abstinence.
> *abstention*: the act of abstaining (e.g. refusal to cast a vote).

Abstinence is often a practice or state, *abstention* a single act. Furthermore, *abstinence* is usually to do with self-restraint from pleasure; *abstention* is not limited so.

See **abstemious.**

abstention: see **abstemiousness**.

abstinence, -cy: see **abstemiousness**.

abstinent: see **abstemious**.

abstract: see **extract**.

abstruse: see **obscure**.

abuse: see **misuse**.

abysmal, abyssal There is no difference between an *abysm* and an *abyss* except that the first is now archaic: both mean anything very deep, an immeasurable chasm, a bottomless gorge or gulf, the depth of the sea, or even hell. One may hear, figuratively, of an *abyss of hopelessness,* etc. *Abysmal* is common in its meaning of *very deep* (usually figurative) and even verges on cliché in *abysmal ignorance*. It is often, but loosely and informally, used to mean merely *very bad*. *Abyssal* is rarer, and can be used literally (especially of ocean depths) or figuratively to mean *unfathomable*.

accede, exceed Confusion may arise from careless pronunciation. Apart from their similarity in sound, these words have nothing in common.

accede (to): agree (to)
exceed: go beyond.
Accede also has the meaning of *enter an office* as in *accede to the throne.*
See **access** and **exceed**.

accept, except *Accept* is a verb with a number of familiar meanings, the commonest of which is *receive*. *Except* is a verb meaning *exclude* (as in *present company excepted*), a preposition meaning *excluding* (*Everyone came except you*) and an old-fashioned conjunction meaning *unless.*
For **except** see also **except** and **exempt**.

access, accession, excess The first two share the general sense of *entering*. The use of *accession* (from **accede**) is limited to a few special contexts. It means *entering upon an office, acceptance of a treaty* (as in Britain's *accession* to the EEC) or *addition (to a collection)*: a library's *accessions* are its acquisitions. *Access* is a more general word meaning *way/act/privilege of approaching or entering*, the emphasis being on the opportunity rather than the act. *Access*, less familiarly, also means *outburst,* and it is important to distinguish between a simple *access of rage* and an *excess* of it, which is too much.

accessary, accessory Variants of the same word meaning *somebody or something incidentally useful*. There used to be a clear distinction between *accessary* (a *person* assisting with an act, usually criminal, as in *an accessary before/after the fact*) and *accessory* (a *thing* that is additional or secondary: the *accessories* to a dress may be matching shoes or gloves, and *car accessories* may include tool-kit or burglar-alarm). American English has always used the *-ory* ending for both senses, and this simplification is now common in British usage – though not common enough to be yet regarded as entirely standard.

accidental, incidental
accidental: happening by chance.
incidental: happening in connexion with something more important. (*The main advantage of having a small car is that it is cheap: an incidental advantage is that it is quickly cleaned.*)
Incidental (up)on means *caused by* (usually but not necessarily by something more important).

accord, account The correct wording is '*of* one's own *accord*' and '*on* one's own *account*'. The first means *of one's own will*, i.e. voluntarily, without prompting. The second means *on one's own responsibility* with the additional sense of *for one's own sake or purposes*.

3

acetic: see **aesthetic**.

acquirement, acquisition   Both mean something gained or the act of gaining it. However, an *acquisition* is a thing or person; an *acquirement* is an ability or accomplishment, such as a mental attainment.

activate, actuate   Both mean *put into action*: a burglar may *activate* or *actuate* an alarm system. Only *actuate*, however, can mean *inspire* or *motivate*, as a person may be *actuated* by the best of intentions. The safest rule is to apply *activate* to things (*central-heating activated by a time-switch*) and *actuate* to people.

acuity, acumen   Both have to do with sharpness. *Acuity* is acuteness of thought or understanding. *Acumen* (pronounced with the accent on the second syllable as in *accuse*) is insight, penetration, good judgement.

adapt, adopt
> *adapt*: change, adjust (to suit different conditions).
> *adopt*: accept (responsibility for); choose; take from someone else.

See also **adaptation**.

adaptation, adoption   The difference is that between **adapt, adopt**:
> *adaptation*:   the act of adapting.
> *adoption*:   the act of adopting.

Confusion may stem from the frequent necessity of making adaptations to something (e.g. a plan) before its adoption, so that adaptation often results in adoption.

There is no such word as *adaption*.

See **adapt** and **adopted**.

adduce, deduce, deduct
> *adduce*: quote as proof or evidence (*The reasons he adduced were unconvincing*).
> *deduce*: draw a conclusion (by reasoning) (*He deduced that they were lying*).
> *deduct*: take away, subtract.

One sometimes hears *deducted* for *deduced*, perhaps because *deduction* is the noun form of both *deduce* and *deduct*. The verb forms, however, are distinct: *deduce, deduced, deducing* and *deduct, deducted, deducting*.

See **induction**.

adhere, cohere

    adhere: stick fast. The world may be used literally (*wallpaper that will not adhere*) or figuratively (*adhere to a belief, group, rule,* etc.).

    cohere: stick together; agree; be consistent.

For the corresponding nouns see **adherence** and **cohesion**.

adherence, adhesion   Both of these nouns mean *the act or state of adhering* (i.e. sticking or holding fast) and they are synonymous in the figurative sense of *devotion* to a cause, religion, etc. However, *adherence* is more usually found in this sense (*adherence to his principles*) and *adhesion* is normally used in the literal sense (*the adhesion of tyres to the road surface*).

See **adhere** and **adherent**.

adherent, adhesive   These may act as adjectives or nouns, and have to do with **adhere**, stick fast. *Adherent* (like **adherence**) is usually found in the figurative sense: it is most common as a noun meaning *supporter* (e.g. of a political party). *Adhesive* (like **adhesion**) is usually literal; glue is an *adhesive* (noun); *adhesive tape* (adjective) is sticky.

See **adhere** and **adherence**.

adjacent, adjoining, contiguous   Often used interchangeably, so much so that many dictionaries give them the same meanings: *neighbouring* or *joined together* (which are not, of course, the same thing). Careful users will discriminate between

    adjoining: joined, touching.

    adjacent: close by.

If two rooms are *adjoining* they are next door or connected: if they are *adjacent* they are merely near to each other.

Contiguous means either, but the primary meaning is *touching, having a common boundary*.

adjure: see **abjure**.

administer: see **minister**.

admission, admittance   The common meaning is *being allowed to enter*, but *admittance* stresses the physical act of entering and the right to enter: it is a rather formal and discouraging word, seen most often on notices saying 'No Admittance'. *Admission* is more familiar and is the general word for entering to join others, e.g. *admission to a school or theatre*. The emphasis is less on physical movement, more on the general sense of participation.

adopt: see **adapt**.

adopted, adoptive   To adopt someone else's child is to accept legal responsibility for his care as one's own. Hence:
>   *adopted*: accepted by adoption.
>   *adoptive*: due to or related by adoption.

A child may be *adopted* or *adoptive*, usually the former. Parents are always *adoptive*.

advance, advancement   Despite their obvious connection, these have distinct meanings:
>   *advance*:   forward movement, progress.
>   *advancement*: promotion (of person or idea, plan, etc.), preferment, furtherance.

A person who makes an *advance* in his studies is making progress; one who seeks *advancement* in his profession wants to move higher.

advantage: see **vantage**.

adventitious, adventurous
>   *adventitious*: happening by accident or chance.
>   *adventurous*: willing to take risks; enterprising.

Only things are *adventitious*. People (and occasionally things, such as ideas and plans) may be *adventurous*.

adventure: see **venture**.

adverse, averse   Remember that *adverse* is not used of people and *averse* usually is.
>   *adverse*: unfavourable, hostile (*adverse publicity, adverse conditions*).
>   *averse*: disinclined, (mildly) opposed (even though *aversion* implies strong dislike) (*She seemed averse to the idea*).

Only *adverse* may be used before a noun. Either may be used after a verb: *public opinion was adverse, I am averse to . . . .*

Both words may be followed by *to*, and *averse* is seldom found without it. The old belief that only *averse from* is correct is no longer held, except by a few purists who recognise its good sense.

Confusion arises because of the common expression *not averse to*, a slightly reluctant way of saying *prepared to accept* or *in favour of*. By analogy, some people say *I'm not adverse to . . . .*, meaning *not hostile to* = in favour of. But this is wrong: people cannot be adverse, only things: see the opening sentence of this entry.

advice, advise Pronounced differently, but sometimes confused in the spelling. *Advice* is the noun, *advise* the verb. If in doubt, think of the word *ice*, which is spelt as it is pronounced.

advisedly, intentionally The common error is to assume that *advisedly* means *after taking advice* and therefore *deliberately* and *intentionally*. The meanings are in fact different:
advisedly: after consideration.
intentionally: on purpose.
It is possible to act intentionally without acting advisedly.

adviser, advisor Alternative spellings, the former being the more usual and the more English.

aeon: see **era**.

aesthetic, ascetic, acetic As adjectives:
aesthetic: relating to the appreciation of beauty; artistic. Pronounced ees–THET-ic.
ascetic: severe in self-denial and rejection of comforts (especially for religious reasons). Pronounced a-SET-ic.
acetic: pertaining to vinegar. Pronounced a-SEE-tic.

affect, effect The idea of impact or influence is common to some of the many meanings of these words: *to affect* can mean *to have an effect*. Confusion is added because the two are often pronounced alike, though *effect* should be said with a distinct *if-*.
Affect exists as a rare noun, but is almost always used as a verb with these meanings:
1. act on or influence, often adversely. *The noise affected his hearing.*
2. move emotionally. *His illness affected her.*
3. imitate, pretend. *He affected indifference.* The adjective *affected* and noun *affectation* are related to this meaning.
Effect is used mainly as a noun, less often as a verb:
1. (noun) result. *The effect of the earthquake.*
2. (noun) influence. *His protests had no effect on her.*
3. (noun) the state of being in operation. *Put a plan into effect.*
4. (verb) bring about. *Effect an improvement.*
The usual confusion is between the first two meanings of *affect* and the first two of *effect*, i.e. in mixing up verb and noun. *It will not effect me* and *It will have no affect* are wrong. To avoid this confusion,

7

afflict, inflict

remember that *affect* has to do with cause and *effect* with result, and that *affect* is nearly always a verb, *effect* usually a noun.

afflict, inflict   Both are associated with suffering.

> *afflict*: cause distress (to someone).
> *inflict*: impose something unpleasant (e.g. defeat, pain, punishment, blows) (on someone).

Generally a person is afflicted with something, and a thing is inflicted on someone.

affluent, effluent

> *affluent* (adjective):   wealthy.
> *effluent* (noun):   liquid waste.

Affluence is abundance: *effluence* is a flowing out.

affront, effrontery

> *affront*:   an open insult.
> *effrontery*: shameless insolence, impudent boldness.

One normally hears of *an* affront but *the* effrontery. A person's effrontery may be also an affront to someone, but two different things are being said there. *Effrontery* is something shown: an *affront* is something received.

Affront may also be a verb. There is no such noun as *affrontery*.

afterward, afterwards   *Afterwards* is the usual word. The other is American, and increasingly found, so much so that some dictionaries now accept it as standard.

aggravate, irritate   *Aggravate* has for centuries been used to mean *irritate* in the sense of *annoy*, but this widespread usage is condemned by those who still want to restrict *aggravate* to its primary meaning of *make worse* (an illness, injury, condition, offence, problem, etc.). The popular usage must still be regarded as colloquial, therefore. It is not wrong, but it is frowned on. Use *aggravate* for *make worse* and *irritate* for *annoy* to be on the safe side.

agnostic, atheist   An *atheist* denies the existence of God. An *agnostic* holds that the existence of God cannot be proved or disproved.

aid, aide   A possible, though admittedly unlikely, source of confusion. One of the rare meanings of the familiar word *aid* is *helper*. An *aide* is also a helper: the word is a short form of the military term *aide-de-camp*, an officer acting as personal assistant to a senior one. It has crept from military and diplomatic circles into some business ones, rather pretentiously.

alias: see **alibi**.

alibi, excuse, alias An *alibi* is a legal defence, or evidence, that a suspect or accused was elsewhere when a crime was committed. Loosely, it has come to mean also a person who is prepared to give eye-witness evidence to that effect on the suspect's behalf.

Even more loosely, it is used to mean an *excuse* (*His alibi for not coming was that he got the date wrong*). This is inexcusable, there being plenty of words that will serve (*defence, justification, pretext, reason, explanation*) without abusing *alibi* in this way. Such mishandling of it is informal if not incorrect: *alibi* has a specific, useful and unique meaning, which is worth preserving intact.

An *alias* is an assumed name. It is not another word for *alibi*, whatever some people may say.

allegory: see **analogy**.

alleviate, ameliorate
  alleviate: make less painful.
  ameliorate: make better, become better.
One may *alleviate* a problem or *ameliorate* a condition. The trades union official who said he wanted to ameliorate a certain problem (i.e. make it into a better problem) perhaps meant that he wanted to alleviate it, though one cannot be sure.

allocate, allot These have in common the sense of *divide into shares*. *Allocate* means *assign for a specific purpose* (as in *The committee allocated funds for the repair of the roof*) and often has to do with *place* (*allocate people to seats*). *Allot* has a stronger sense of *share*. People may have tickets or time allotted to them; the implication is that the allotment is from a larger number or amount.

allowed, aloud
  allowed: permitted.
  aloud: out loud.

all ready, already
  all ready (adjective): completely ready.
  already (adverb):   by a particular time; as early as this.
The first is to be used when the emphasis is on readiness. *Are we all*

all right, alright

ready? We're already late. The knives and forks are *already/all ready on the table.*

all right, alright   However often it may appear in print – and it appears frequently – *alright* is not standard, as the dictionaries which deign to include it invariably point out. Its time may come, but until then it is safer to stick with *all right*, the traditionally correct form.

all together, altogether
> *all together*:   all in or to one place; all at the same time; all co-operating, connecting or united.
> *altogether*:   in total; completely; on the whole.

To eat four ice-creams *altogether* (in total) is quite a different matter from eating them *all together* (simultaneously).

allude, refer   Commonly thought to mean the same, but they do not. If you *allude* to something, you *refer* to it indirectly, incidentally, in passing.
> See **elude**.

allure: see **lure**.

allusion, illusion, delusion   Both *illusion* and *delusion* denote a false or misleading experience, perception or belief, but an *illusion* is a mild state of deception, a *delusion* being deeper, usually unreasonable, and often harmful. A foolish person may have (or be under) the *illusion* or *delusion* that he is wise: the latter simply implies a more extreme degree of self-deception.

Illusion has the additional meaning of a false or deceptive *appearance* or the false impression created by it. Thus a magician deals in illusions (and, confusingly, *deludes* his audience: there is a verb *illude* corresponding to *illusion* but it is seldom used, and *delude* does duty for all the senses of *create illusion/delusion*).

An *allusion* is an indirect reference: see **allude**.

allusive, elusive
> *allusive*:   referring indirectly; hinting. See **allude**.
> *elusive*:   difficult to discover, recall, pin down, catch; designed to avoid.

The *-lusive* part of the words has to do with play. The prefixes mean *at/around* and *away from* respectively.

all ways, always
> *all ways*:   every method; every respect.
> *always*:   every time; repeatedly; in any case.

If *ways* has the force of a separate noun (*in all ways*; *I have tried all ways*) it must be written separately.

aloud: see **allowed**.

already: see **all ready**.

alright: see **all right**.

altar, alter
> *altar* (noun): place where religious rites are performed.
> *alter* (verb): make or become different.

alternate, alternative   As an adjective, *alternate* (pronounced with the stress on the second syllable: the verb has the stress on the first) means *occurring by turns, first one then the other*. If a person works on alternate days, he works for a day, has the next day off, and then repeats the pattern. A magazine that appears in alternate months is published every other month.

Alternative, also as an adjective, means *affording a choice*. It used to be restricted to *offering a choice between only two*, but this limitation no longer applies. *There is an alternative way of doing it* means that there is a choice of method. *Alternative* always implies choice.

For this reason, it is loose to use it as a showy substitute for *other* when no choice is available. *We shall have to make alternative arrangements* should mean (though it seldom does) *We shall have to make two (or more) sets of arrangements* (implying *and then decide which is best*). It should not mean *We shall have to make other/different arrangements* (implying *because we have no choice*), though that is how most people would use it.

It is now common for *alternative* also to mean *unconventional* (as in *alternative theatre*, etc.).

In America this distinction between *alternate* and *alternative* is not observed.

alternately, alternatively   The difference is the same as that in **alternate, alternative**:
> *alternately*:   by turns. *He comes on Mondays and Wednesdays alternately* i.e. on Monday one week, Wednesday the next, then Monday, etc.
> *alternatively*: as a matter of choice. *You can take a bus; alternatively, there is a train-service*, i.e. you can choose.

although, though *Though* can always be a substitute for *although*, but the converse is not true. Only *though* is possible in *as though* . . . and *even though* . . . and in the (rather informal) adverbial sense of *however* (*I did my best, though*).

Although is more formal, perhaps a shade stronger, and still recommended at the beginning of a sentence, though *though* is in much more general use.

altogether: see **all together**.

always: see **all ways**.

ambiance, ambience Alternative spellings; both refer to the atmosphere of a place as created by the surroundings. *Ambiance* has been imported from French and is pronounced (roughly) 'am-bi-ornce'. *Ambience* is English and preferable, pronounced 'ambi-ence'.

amatory, amorous Both mean *pertaining to (sexual) love*, but *amorous* is the more common word, *amatory* tending to be confined to what is written (*amatory poetry*).

ambiguous, ambivalent
    ambiguous: having more than one *meaning*. Only things (what people say, write, do, etc.) can be *ambiguous*.
    ambivalent: having two (or more) conflicting *feelings* about the same thing or person. Only people can be *ambivalent*, though what they say, do, etc., can show *ambiguity*.
  Both words are used very loosely, and interchangeably, as if they meant no more than *vague, undecided*, etc.
  It is possible for a statement to both be *ambiguous* (unclear) and show *ambivalence* (express opposing attitudes), but the words have quite separate meanings and should be used with respect.

ameliorate: see **alleviate**.

amend, emend Both have the sense of *alter in order to make better*. To *amend* is to improve, as Parliament amends legislation. To *emend* is more specifically to correct a text.
  The corresponding nouns are *amendment* and *emendation*.

amiable, amicable Both mean *friendly* but *amiable* is applied to people and their disposition, *amicable* to things, such as conversations or agreements.

amid, amidst   Either will do, but the second is old-fashioned and seldom used nowadays. *Amid* is rather formal, *in the middle of* being usually preferred in speech, but this is not always possible: *He resigned amid protests/objections/speculation . . .* etc.

ammunition, munitions   *Ammunition* is normally thought of as anything that can be discharged from a gun, plane, ship, gas-canister, etc. as a means of attack or defence. Figuratively it can be applied to material deployed in an argument.
  Munitions is a more general word embracing all war equipment and stores, including ammunition.

amok, amuck   Both words have the same meaning, and are found almost exclusively in the expression *to run amok/amuck*, to go about behaving in a frenzied way. It can be applied literally to, say, an armed man going berserk, or figuratively to other sorts of havoc, such as share-prices running out of control.
  Both spellings are acceptable; the former is more usual (the latter used to be) which is a pity: both the sound and appearance of *amuck* have merit even though the word has nothing whatsoever to do with *muck*.

among, amongst   Variants of the same word. The latter is sometimes dismissed as archaic as well as unnecessary, but it lingers quite strongly, and is blameless, apart from being a shade longer than the other.

amoral, immoral, unethical
  amoral: having no morals; unconcerned or unconnected with moral standards; having no moral standards – good or bad – by which one can be judged.
  immoral: having bad morals; not with conforming or opposed to moral standards; wicked; the opposite of moral.
  unethical: not in conformity with the rules of right behaviour within a profession. For the difference between morals and ethics see **ethic**.

amorous: see **amatory**.

amount, number, quantity   *Amount* refers to *quantity* reckoned in mass or bulk (*a large amount of bread*), *number* to quantity reckoned in separate items (*a large number of sandwiches*). A *quantity* may therefore be an amount or a number, but it is careless to assume that *amount*

13

amuck

means *number*: one can no more have *a small amount of chairs* than *a small number of furniture*. The general rule is *amount* + singular noun, *number* + plural noun, *quantity* + either.

amuck: see **amok**.

analogous: see **similar, synonymous**.

analogy, allegory   Both have to do with parallelism, but
    analogy: agreement or likeness between things that have certain things in common but are otherwise different.
    allegory: literary or artistic work in which what is represented has a deeper or concealed meaning (e.g. moral, spiritual, political); the use of that sort of symbolism.
One may draw an *analogy* between love and madness. *Pilgrim's Progress* and *1984* are allegories.
   See **similar**.

annex, annexe   *Annex* has customarily been the verb (meaning *add to something* as when a country takes over territory as its own), *annexe* the noun (meaning *something added*, such as a building extension or a supplement added to a document). *Annexe* is now losing ground (perhaps under the influence of American English, which has always preferred *annex* as both verb and noun) and it is now common to find *annex* used as a noun in all the senses of *annexe*. A supplementary building is still more likely to be called an *annexe*, but here too *annex* is now permitted.
   See **appendix**.

announce, pronounce   In the sense of *make known*, *announce* is the general word. To *pronounce* is to declare officially, formally, authoritatively (or pompously).

annual, perennial
    annual: happening every year (*an annual event*); lasting for a year (*annual permission*).
    perennial: lasting for a year or longer; everlasting; perpetually recurring (*perennial problem*).
A plant that is an *annual* lasts for a year, a *perennial* for several years.

antagonist, protagonist
    antagonist: opponent.
    protagonist: chief person (in play, etc.); important advocate of a cause.

14

Protagonist is often used to mean merely *supporter*. This is very loose: the idea of *chief* must be present (and the adjectives in *chief/main/principal protagonists* are redundant). The old insistence that there can be only one protagonist no longer holds, but it is a useful reminder of the strength and uniqueness of the word, which should not be debased by being used as a fancy substitute for *campaigner*.

The Prime Minister and Leader of the Opposition, as *protagonists* in a debate, are likely to be *antagonists* too. That does not mean—as is often thought—that the words mean the same. *Antagonist* implies antagonism: *protagonist* does not and cannot.

ante-, anti- The prefixes have distinct meanings:
> *ante-*: before, in front of (as in *antecedent*).
> *anti-*: against, opposite, reverse (as in *antidote*).

The pronunciation of *anti-* with the second syllable as *eye* is exclusively American.

anticipate, expect The special meaning of *anticipate* is *foresee and forestall* (so that *to anticipate a difficulty* is to be aware of it in advance and take appropriate steps to deal with it) and *act before the proper time* (as an athlete may *anticipate the starting-gun*).

Some people regret that it has also come to be no more than a showy alternative to *expect* in its sense of *regard as likely*. It is a pity (and still regarded as loose in some quarters) that *anticipate* in this sense merely duplicates another word, and in a way that may be ambiguous: does *I anticipated that there would be objections* mean simply that I regarded them as likely or that I was additionally ready to deal with them?

Only *expect* can be followed by an infinitive (*He expects to fail*) or mean *require* (*I expect good service*).

antiquated, antique
> *antiquated*: old-fashioned to the extent of being useless, or nearly so.
> *antique*: old-fashioned to the extent of being valuable.

antisocial: see **unsociable**.

any more, anymore The second is American and is incorrect in British English, where *any more* is invariable.

any one, anyone *Anyone* means *any person. Any one* must be used when *one* is a numeral and *any* means *whichever*, as *Please pass me any one of those newspapers.*

15

any way, anyway   When the emphasis is on *way*, and *any* is clearly adjectival, use *any way*: *I can't agree in any way. Do it any way you can.* In the more throwaway sense of *in any case* use *anyway*: *Anyway, I can't be there.*

apology, apologia   An *apology* is an expression of regret for something, with or without an explanation. An *apologia* is a more formally stated (often written or published) defence or vindication of belief, behaviour, a cause, etc. *Apology* may also be used in this sense.

appendix, annex   Both these words refer to supplementary material at the end of a book or document, such as statistical tables or detailed background information which would break up or disturb the flow of the main body of writing, but which needs to be included for those readers wanting access to it. *Appendix* (plural *appendices* or *appendixes*) is the usual name for an addition to a book; an *annex* (or *annexe*) is more usually found at the end of a report, though *appendix* is quite normal.
   See **annex**.

apposite: see **opposite**.

appraise: see **apprise**.

appreciable, appreciative   These come from two differing senses of *appreciate*:
   appreciable: capable of being estimated or measured.
   appreciative: feeling or showing gratitude.

apprehend, reprehend, comprehend   In its sense of *grasp* (mentally or physically) *apprehend* can mean *understand*, as can *comprehend*, though *apprehend* is rather flowery in this sense. But there is no excuse for any confusion with *reprehend* (*blame*). The familiar adjectival forms are *comprehensible* (understandable), *comprehensive* (all-inclusive), *apprehensive* (fearful) and *reprehensible* (blameworthy).

apprise, appraise   Frequently confused.
   apprise: inform (person *of* something).
   appraise: assess value of.
   Perhaps the confusion arises because an *appraisal* (evaluation) or *reappraisal* may be pieces of *information*. Be that as it may, *to be appraised of* is never right, though *to be apprised of* (to be told about) is common and correct. You may appraise a person (and then apprise

16

him of your appraisal) but you are more likely to appraise his performance, efficiency, etc.

approve: see **endorse**.

apt: see **likely**.

arbiter, arbitrator   Both of these **arbitrate**, i.e. make a decision, but in different ways. An *arbiter* has absolute control over a decision: an *arbitrary decision* is a dictatorial one. An *arbitrator* is a person (usually appointed because he is independent, often by the agreement of both sides) who settles a dispute by hearing evidence and then making a decision. He usually operates officially (e.g. in industrial disputes) but on *arbiter* is anyone who sets himself up as judge.

See **arbitrate**.

arbitrate, mediate   To *arbitrate* is to come to a decision, usually to settle a dispute, by a formal or official process of hearing argument or evidence from the parties in disagreement. To *mediate* is simply to act or intervene as a go-between, again usually in a dispute, but as a means of communication, not as a judge (though the intention is usually to reconcile).

See **arbiter**.

arise, rise   *Rise* has numerous meanings, mostly associated with upward movement: *rise from one's bed, soldier rises through the ranks, river rises in the mountains, people rose in rebellion, sun/prices/voices rose, cakes rise in cooking.*

Arise used to have some of those meanings (*I will arise and go to my father*) but it now almost always means *come into being, originate, become apparent* (as in *The question doesn't arise; the problem arose; the matter has arisen*) without any sense of upward or physical movement.

See **rise**.

armoury, arsenal   In the sense of *a collection of or storehouse for arms and other military equipment*, either *armoury* or *arsenal* will do, though *armoury* tends to be used of a designated storehouse on a military base and *arsenal* of a collection (*The police-raid uncovered an arsenal of weapons in the garage of the house*). An *armoury* is additionally a permanent display of (usually old) weaponry in, say, a castle, and *arsenal* is also a place where weapons are manufactured.

Both words are used figuratively to mean a repertory of things (e.g. arguments, word-power, footballing skills) that can be used to one's

around

advantage in a confrontation; *armoury* is probably the more common in such usage.

around: see **round**.

arouse: see **rouse**.

arrogate: see **abrogate**.

arsenal: see **armoury**.

artful: see **arty**.

artist, artiste   *Artiste* is a pretentious word for a public performer (especially a singer or actor), so much that it is now used only in comic contexts as if mocking the grandiloquent flourishes of the circus tent or music hall. *Artist* is the only straight-faced term for a public performer, or a practitioner in any art-form.

arty, artful   *Arty* is a rather dismissive term to describe someone pretentiously artistic, affecting the imagined extravagant behaviour or appearance of an artist without necessarily having his talent. *Artful*: skilfully cunning.

ascendancy, ascendant   The usual phrases, meaning *to have dominant position or influence*, are *to have the ascendancy* and *to be in the ascendant*, though the latter is fast coming to mean *to have increasing dominance, to be on the way up*, which must now be accepted as standard.

ascetic: see **aesthetic**.

Asian, Asiatic   Synonyms both as nouns and adjectives, but the latter is now seldom found, and is thought by some authorities to be pejorative, even racist. *Asian* is unexceptionable.

assault, assail   Both mean *attack*, but in practice *assault* is usually literal and physical, *assail* figurative and abstract. An audience may *assail* a speaker with questions or objections so that he is *assailed* (disturbed, overwhelmed) by doubts, anxiety, etc.

assay, essay   As verbs, both mean *try*, but *assay* is now almost always restricted to *analyse* in the strict sense of finding out how much gold or silver there is in an artefact or coin, bullion, etc. *Essay* is more common but rather pedantic; the simpler *try* or *try out* is preferable.

assent, consent   Both mean *agree*, but *consent* has the additional sense

18

of *give permission* after having been asked, which may imply the existence of some reflection before agreement. *Assent* therefore implies readier agreement.

assignment, assignation Both are from the verb *assign* (appoint, allocate, set apart for a purpose):
    assignment: task, duty allotted to one.
    assignation: appointment to meet (usually secret, often between lovers).

assume, presume Both have many different meanings, but they come close together (and are often used as synonyms) in the sense of *suppose, take for granted*. *Assume* is the more tentative word and implies supposition without evidence. *Presume* is more positive and implies a greater degree of certainty.

    The corresponding nouns *assumption* and *presumption* have the same colourings.

assurance, insurance To make an arrangement to receive money in the event of a person's death is to have *assurance*, but one takes out *insurance* against all other risks, such as the theft or the destruction by fire of household goods. The distinction seems pointless, but it exists.

assure, ensure, insure
    assure: convince; state earnestly, guarantee; make (person or thing) sure.
    ensure: make (thing) certain.
    So *I was assured*, not *I was ensured*. *He ensured* (made certain) *that the car was working* but *He assured* (convinced, promised) *me that it was working*. Success may be *assured* or *ensured*, the former being a little stronger. Idiom requires *They ensured that . . .* , not *They assured that . . .* and either *I assured myself that . . .* or *I ensured that . . .* , which mean the same.
    Insure: guarantee against loss, etc. through paying insurance. For the difference between insurance and assurance, see **assurance**.

astrology, astronomy
    astrology: supposed science of influence of stars on human affairs and world happenings.
    astronomy: scientific study of planets and stars.

astronaut, cosmonaut An *astronaut* is an American space-man; a *cosmonaut* is a Russian one.

atheist

The -*naut* part means *sailor*; the other parts mean *star* and *universe* respectively.

atheist: see **agnostic**.

atmosphere, stratosphere
> *atmosphere*: gaseous layer surrounding earth (or other heavenly body).
>
> *stratosphere*: layer of the atmosphere between about seven and fifty miles up. The troposphere is below it, the ionosphere outside it.

auger, augur
> *auger* (noun): tool for boring.
>
> *augur* (verb): foresee, portend. Usually found in *it augurs well/badly*, it appears to promise success/failure.
>
> See also **augury**.

augury, auspice   Both mean *omen, indication, portent*, but an *auspice* is usually favourable. These are uncommon words, though the plural *auspices* in the expression *under the auspices of* (under the patronage of, organised by) is familiar.
> See also **auger** and **auspicious**.

aural, oral, verbal   These pertain, in order, to the ear, the mouth, and words.
> *aural*: relating to the ear or hearing. An *aural* examination may be a test of one's hearing or of one's understanding of what one has heard.
>
> *oral*: relating to the mouth or the spoken word. An *oral* exam is a test of one's ability to speak (e.g. a foreign language) in response to spoken questions. *Oral medicine* is swallowed, not injected, etc.
>
> *verbal*: relating to words. Strictly speaking, *verbal communication* is communication in words rather than by drawings, signs, signals, etc. Its common use to mean the same as *oral* (*He left a verbal message*, i.e. not a written one, but by word of mouth or telephone) hovers between the loose and the (barely) acceptable. Why not avoid ambiguity and say *oral message*, leaving *verbal* to mean what it really means?

Aural and *oral* are normally pronounced with the first syllable as in *organ*, though the *o-* in *oral* may rhyme with that in *pot*. Fortunately *aural* is little used outside schools, so ambiguity seldom arises.

auspicious, propitious   There is little to choose between these two, which mean *favourable, conducive to success*, though usage sometimes prefers one rather than the other: one is more likely to say *propitious weather* and *an auspicious beginning* than the other way round.

The use of *auspicious* to mean no more than *important*, as in the speech-maker's hackneyed *on this auspicious occasion*, is loose if not incorrect.

See **augury**.

autarchy, autarky   Pronounced alike, but
    autarchy: absolute power; autocracy.
    autarky: self-sufficiency (usually economic).
See **autocracy**.

authoritative, authoritarian
    authoritative: having or using authority; commanding; expert, reliable (*an authoritative text-book/tone of voice/manner/judgement*, etc.).
    authoritarian: imposing (one's own) authority; dictatorial; favouring obedience to authority rather than individual freedom (*an authoritarian regime/headmaster* etc.).

The first has a positive feel, implying respect; the second has a negative feel, implying reservation.

autocracy, autonomy
    autocracy: dictatorship.
    autonomy: self-government.

The corresponding adjectives are *autocratic* (despotic) and *autonomous* (self-governing, independent).

avenge, revenge   These verbs mean *inflict punishment for injury received*. The difference, largely ignored in everyday usage, is that *avenge* carries the implication of action in the interests of justice whereas *revenge* carries that of getting one's own back, sometimes in retaliation for an injury that may be disproportionately small or even imagined. *Avenge* therefore signifies honour: *revenge* signifies spite.

One may *avenge* another person (e.g. a friend, by punishing whomever wronged him) or an injury (e.g. a defeat at football, by winning the next match). One usually revenges oneself; one cannot

21

avenge oneself. The usual constructions are that one may *be avenged* or (less commonly) *revenge oneself*.

For the corresponding nouns see **vengeance, revenge**.

averse: see **adverse**.

avocation: see **vocation**.

avoidance, evasion

> *avoidance*: the act of keeping away from someone or something. Shunning.
>
> *evasion*: escape by trickery, cunning or dishonesty.

Tax *avoidance* is legitimate: there are various lawful means of using one's money to avoid paying tax on it. Tax *evasion* is illegal.

See **evade** and **evasion**.

await: see **wait**.

awake, wake, awaken, waken All mean the same (*emerge or rouse from sleep or other inactivity*). All can be used literally (i.e. of sleep) or figuratively (i.e. of other inactivity). All can be used with or without an object. It is something of a nightmare to pick one's way through them but here are the simplest rules:

1. *Wake* (woke, woken) is the usual form. It is the only one that can be used with *up*. Examples with direct object: *Wake him up*; *they woke him*; *they have woken him up*. Examples without direct object: *I woke up*; *I was woken by the noise*. This is the safest form to stick to.
2. *Awake* (awoke, awoken) and especially *awaken* (awakened) are generally used figuratively in the sense of *rouse*: *to awaken suspicion*; *a rude awakening*.
3. *Awake* as an adjective means *not asleep* (*I was wide awake*) and *alert* (*He was awake to the danger*).
4. *Waken* (wakened) is probably the most old-fashioned of the four and, like *awaken*, is used figuratively more than literally.
5. *Awaken* and *waken* are often found in the passive: *she was awakened (or wakened)* (or, better, *woken (up)*) *by* . . .
6. *Awake* (as verb) and *waken* are the most dispensible of the four.
7. As a working rule, stay with *wake* (up), using *awaken* (awakened) and perhaps *awake* for figurative purposes.

award, reward The idea of giving something is central to both, but the circumstances of the giving are different.

> *award*: something officially given by way of recognition, as a prize or penalty.
>
> *reward*: something given by way of recompense or return for service or merit.

The notion of reciprocation always accompanies *reward*.

The verb-forms have differing constructions. You *award* something *to* somebody, but *reward* someone *with* something or *reward* something (e.g. effort) *by* giving something. You may be awarded a prize or be rewarded *with* a prize.

aware: see **unaware**.

awhile, a while

> *awhile* (adverb): *for* a *short* period of time. (*We waited awhile, then went home*).
>
> *a while* (noun): a period of time.

A while may be a long period of time (*We waited (for) quite a while*) though the normal implication is that it is short (*We can only wait for a while*). When *while* is a noun it must be written as a separate word, e.g. following a preposition (*after a while*), adverb (*quite a while*) or adjective (*a short while*). For *awhile* and *quite awhile* make no sense.

axiom: see **maxim**.

B

backward, backwards Only *backward* may be used adjectivally: *a backward step*. Either may be used adverbially: *move backward*; *bend over backwards*. Perhaps *backwards* is the more popular.

bail, bale *Bale* is invariable in the sense of a bundle (*a bale of straw*) or package. See also **baleful**.

  Bail is invariable in all the senses connected with the legal arrangements for paying money as a surety that someone will appear in court. You can literally *bail out* a person in this way or, figuratively, help someone out of other difficulties (*The bank bailed us out with a loan*). The cricketing term is *bails*.

  Either *bale* or *bail* will serve for *make an emergency exit* (especially from an aircraft) or *remove water* (especially from a boat). There is a faint preference for *bale* for the former and *bail* for the latter (though

baited

American English, perversely, puts things the other way round), but it matters little.

Confusingly, some argue that the idea of *bailing* someone out of a problem comes not from legal *bail* but from the idea of jumping out of a doomed aircraft (*bailing* or *baling*, preferably *baling* – see above), in which case *The bank baled us out with a loan*. But *bailed* is better.

baited: see **bated**.

baleful, baneful   The first derives from an archaic noun *bale* meaning *evil* or *misery*, the second from *bane* (meaning *something that causes distress or destruction*), usually found only in the expression *the bane of my life*.

Both mean *exercising a harmful or destructive influence* so that it is possible to speak of alcohol's *baneful* or *baleful* effect, the former being stronger. That apart, *baleful* is often used to describe a stare or look in the sense of *threatening, malignant, vengeful*. *Baneful* means *ruinous, evil, poisonous*.

balk: see **baulk**.

balmy, barmy   *Balmy* is an uncommon word, usually applied to weather to signify that it is mild and pleasant, though the literal meaning, from *balm*, is *fragrant*. *Barmy* is popular slang (though uncommon in having remained so for far longer than most slang words) for *silly* or *mad*.

Under the influence of American English, which has always used *balmy* for all the above meanings, that spelling is now recognised by some dictionaries as an alternative to *barmy* in British English. It is rare, however, non-standard and unnecessary.

baneful: see **baleful**.

barbarian, barbaric, barbarous   All signify lack of culture, in different degrees. *Barbarian* is usually a noun denoting an uncouth person, though it can be an adjective meaning *uncivilised*. *Barbaric* (crude, in bad taste) is stronger, though it can be used with an air of pained tolerance to describe, say, modern architecture or American food. *Barbarous* is by far the harshest term, meaning *cruel, brutal*.

bare, bear   As verbs:
> *bare*: uncover (*bare one's chest* or *soul*).
> *bear*: carry, tolerate (*bear scrutiny* or *a grudge*).

barmy: see **balmy**.

base, basis Both mean *foundation or fundamental part; bottom or supporting part. Base* is normally used literally (*the base of the skull/structure/mixture*) and *basis* figuratively or theoretically (*the basis of the agreement/argument/problem*).

Basis is often over-used, redundant (*on a weekly basis* instead of simply *weekly*) and incorrect (*on the basis of* does not mean *because of*).

bated, baited *Bated* comes from *bate* meaning *restrain* as in *with bated breath* (in suspense); it is also a variant of *abated* (i.e. *reduced*). *Baited* comes from *bait*, the most common meanings of which are *persecute, tease* and *put food on hook or trap* to tempt animals.

bath, bathe, bathing English people *bath* in a bath, *bathe* in the sea or a swimming-pool (though Americans do so in a bathroom), and *bathe* a wound by cleaning it with liquid.

Bathing (and *bathed*) relate to either word but the pronunciation differs in the way the pronunciation of *bath* and *bathe* does.

bathos, pathos
> *bathos*: ludicrous anticlimax by sudden descent from dignity or intensity to the commonplace, in speech, writing or a happening.
> *pathos*: quality (in art or an event) that creates feelings of pity or sadness.

Loosely, *bathos* can also be used to mean false *pathos*, i.e. embarrassing sentimentality.

The corresponding adjectives are *bathetic* and *pathetic*, the latter having also an informal sense of *derisory, unsatisfying, contemptibly weak*.

baulk, balk Alternative spellings, the first being more common except in America. Found usually, though not exclusively, as a verb meaning *thwart* (*His plans were baulked by his superiors*) or *hold back in the face of difficulty* (*He baulked at the idea of . . .*). The pronunciation usually rhymes with *walk*, but it is not incorrect to sound the *l*.

There are signs that the spelling *balk* is becoming more popular, perhaps by sensible analogy with *talk, walk*, etc.

bear: see **bare**.

begrudge, grudge Often used interchangeably, which is no great sin, but there is a slight difference in emphasis.

begrudge: envy (person) the possession of (thing).

grudge: give or allow (thing) reluctantly to (person); to look upon enviously.

The first, then, suggests envy, the second unwillingness or envy. Only *grudge* is a noun meaning *feeling of resentment*.

bellicose, belligerent   Two nations that are *belligerents* are at war. Figuratively, a *belligerent* person or one who behaves *belligerently* acts as if he were waging war, i.e. in an aggressive or hostile manner. *Bellicose* means *eager to fight* or *pugnacious*; it is a slightly milder term, and may imply mere bluster.

benevolent, beneficent, beneficial, benign

benevolent: wishing to do good; being well-disposed.

beneficent: doing good, giving charity, being generous. (It is people who are usually *beneficent*.)

beneficial: advantageous. (It is things that are usually *beneficial*.)

benign: kindly. (People or things may be *benign*.)

bereaved, bereft   Both mean *deprived* but *bereaved* invariably means *deprived by death* and *bereft* has a more general application: *bereft of any sense of humour, bereft of her senses*.

The fact that the two words used to mean the same is remembered in the occasional use of *bereft* to mean *anguished by loss through death*.

beside, besides   As prepositions, these have distinct meanings:

beside: next to (*Sit beside me*): compared with; irrelevant (*Beside the point*). Also *beside oneself*, overwrought.

besides: in addition to (*Nobody will be there besides us*).

In addition, *besides* can act as an adverb meaning *anyway, moreover* (*Besides, it's too far*).

bi-, by-, by, bye   Confusion arises from their identical pronunciation, and there are some similarities in meaning.

bi- (prefix):   twice, double (*bilingual, bicycle*).

by- (prefix):   near (*bystander*); secondary, incidental (*byway, by-product*). (Check dictionary for hyphens).

by (adverb):   near (*standing by*); past (*The bus went by*), etc.

bye (noun):   something incidental (*leg-bye(s)* in cricket). In a competition a team may enter the second round having had a *bye* (no opponent) in the first.

Note *by and by* (eventually) but *by the bye*

(incidentally). Also *bye-bye*, *'bye*, *goodbye*, versions of *God be with you*.

biannual, biennial

    biannual: occurring twice a year.
    biennial: occurring once in two years; lasting two years.
See **bi-**.

billion, trillion   In Britain, a *billion* is traditionally a million million, whereas in America it is a thousand million. This is obviously confusing to those who routinely deal in such sums, and so the American definition is now normal in the UK; certainly journalists and economists use *billion* to mean a thousand million.

The American term for a million million is *trillion*, which is likewise supplanting the British trillion (a million million million). Not that these distinctions mean much to ordinary people, who have difficulty in imagining them, and seldom need to use these words anyway. All that most people need to know is that a *billion* is very much more than a million, and it little matters whether it is a thousand or a million times more.

blanch, blench   Despite their historical relationship, their current meanings are unambiguously distinct:
    blanch: make white (*blanch vegetables by scalding*); become white
           (*He blanched*, he went pale).
    blench: flinch, quail (*He blenched at the thought*, he drew
           back/hesitated/was fearful, etc.).
Obviously the same event may cause a person to *blanch* or *blench* or do both at the same time, but the words do not mean the same thing.

blatant, flagrant   Popularly used as if they meant the same, especially by politicians and journalists who prefer strong words to important distinctions. Both have the sense of *conspicuous* and *offensive*, but each has a clear and useful emphasis. In *blatant* it is on *conspicuous*, *glaringly obvious*; in *flagrant* it is on *offensive*, *scandalous*.

Flagrant is the stronger, tending towards *evil*. In *a blatant violation of human rights* the stress is on an openness which is also shameful; in a *flagrant violation* . . . the stress is on a wickedness which is also undisguised. A blatant lie is therefore different from a flagrant one.

blench: see **blanch**.

blessed, blest   Alternative forms, the first pronounced as two syllables

27

blond, blonde

when an adjective (*a blessed nuisance*) but otherwise, like *blest*, as one (*She was blessed with good luck*). *Blessed* is generally preferred in writing.

blond, blonde   A woman with light-coloured hair is *blonde* but a man is *blond*. The unisex adjective is *blond*; a *blond race* is a race of people with fair hair and a light complexion. A *blonde* (noun) is a woman with these characteristics.

bludgeon: see **cudgel**.

blush, flush   As both nouns and verbs, these have to do with reddening of the cheeks, but a *blush* is induced by modesty, confusion or shame, a *flush* by much stronger emotion such as anger.
   There are other usages having nothing to do with red, such as *flushed with success* (triumphant, excited) and *at first blush* (at first glance).

board, bored   The first is usually a noun (*board and lodgings*, etc.), the second always a verb (*bored a hole; bored to death*).

bogy, bogey, bogie   No two dictionaries agree about these, so it is just as well that they are not much needed. *Bogey* will do for all three; otherwise plump for:
   bogy: goblin; bugbear.
   bogey: one stroke above par in golf.
   bogie: pivoted undercarriage; trolley.
   All rhyme with *fogey* (or *fogy*!).

boiled, broiled   In cookery, ingredients are *boiled* in hot water or *broiled* by direct heat from a grill, etc. In the sun, you may *boil* or *broil*: in the first case you are (uncomfortably) hot, in the second you are being burned.

bore, boor   A person who wearies one with tediousness is a *bore* (rhymes with *door*). A person who is ill-bred in his manner, or coarse in his expression or opinion, is a *boor* (rhymes with *poor*).

bored: see **board**.

born, borne   Pronounced identically, but *borne* is the correct spelling for *carried* (*In his absence, the responsibility was borne by . . .*) and *impressed* (*It was borne in upon them . . .* They were (gradually) made to realise . . .).
   Born has to do with birth (*a born optimist*).

brake: see **break**.

bravado, bravery, bravura   Aspects of courage. *Bravery* is the real thing. *Bravado* is an act or show of bravery, often no more than boastful threatening, designed to impress. *Bravura* is genuinely impressive – any brilliant, spirited or daring display, especially in a performance (e.g. in music, oratory or on the stage).

breach, breech   These never mean the same, despite identical pronunciation.

By far the more common is *breach* which means a *break*, literally (A *breach in the dam*) or metaphorically (*breach of discipline/confidence/contract/the peace*; *a breach in their relationship/friendship*). A *breech* is the back or lower part of something, often a gun: hence *breeches* (trousers), *breeches-buoy* (apparatus worn like breeches) and *breech birth* (buttocks or feet first).

break, brake   Use *brake* for *slow down or stop*, and *break* in all other cases.

breath, breathe   It is easy to say that *breath* is the noun (*out of breath*) and *breathe* the verb (*breathe in*) but less easy for weak spellers to remember the difference. Perhaps it helps that *breathe*, pronounced with an *-ee-* sound (as in *seethe*), needs to be written with a final *-e*. *Breath* rhymes with *death*.

breech: see **breach**.

Britain, Briton   (Great) *Britain* is the country, a *Briton* its inhabitant, though *Briton* is found only in history before the Roman conquest, in poetry, and in the popular tabloid press for whom it is conveniently shorter than *British person*. In real life nobody calls himself a Briton. See **British**.

British, English   The *English* live in England, the *British* in the United Kingdom of Great Britain (England, Wales, Scotland) and Northern Ireland. The *British* include the *English*, but the English do not include the Welsh, etc.

Most of these, however, speak *English* or (if you must) British English.

Briton: see **Britain**.

broach, brooch   Pronounced alike. A *brooch* is an ornament of dress. Otherwise use *broach* (noun and verb) as in *broach a subject*, etc.

broil: see **boil**.

brooch: see **broach**.

bundle, bungle
> *Manchester United bungled Watford out of the F.A.Cup last evening.*
>> *bundle*: dispatch (person) quickly or unceremoniously.
>> *bungle*: commit a blunder; fail to accomplish successfully.

by: see **bi-**.

bye: see **bi-**.

by heart, by rote If you know something *by heart* you know it perfectly, even though you may never have tried to learn it; for example, you may know a certain route by heart (i.e. without having to look at a map) simply because you have followed it frequently. If you learn something *by rote*, however, you do so deliberately, mechanically, by constant repetition. You may not necessarily understand it, however.

C

cachet, cache Two useful importations from French.
> *cachet*: distinguishing mark, sign of distinction; prestige.
> *cache*: hidden store, especially of weapons or treasure.
> Pronounced *cash-ay* and *cash*.

caddie, caddy Either will do for the person who carries a golfer's clubs, or for the corresponding verb, but only *caddy* is a container for tea.

callous, callus *Callous* is usually encountered as an adjective meaning *unfeeling, insensitive* (as in *callous behaviour*). The literal meaning, used of skin, is *hardened*. There is a verb *callous* meaning *make (skin) hard*, usually found in the passive: *His hands were calloused.*
> *Callus* (same pronounciation) is a noun for *thickened part of skin*, for example on the hands as a result of hard work or on the soles of feet by rubbing in exercise.

callow: see **shallow**.

candelabrum, candelabra, chandelier An ornamental branched candle holder, used as a table decoration, is strictly speaking a *candelabrum* (plural *candelabra*) though nowadays it is generally called a *candelabra* (plural *candelabras*). When hung from the ceiling, usually in much bigger and more elaborate form, it usually (but not necessarily) is called a *chandelier*, even though electricity is now the more normal form of lighting.

cannon, canon Use *cannon* if the context is guns or snooker, *canon* if it is ecclesiastical or musical. A *canon* is also a standard of judgement (*canons of good taste*) or a list of genuine works by a writer, artist, etc.
   Cannon (*into*) is also a verb meaning *collide with*: *cannon against* means *collide with and bounce off*.

canvas, canvass *Canvas* is the material used for tents, sails, etc. A *canvass* is a soliciting of votes, a questioning of people about their opinions, behaviour, etc., or an investigation, usually through discussion.
   Both are also verbs, but only the second is normally used in this way.

capability: see **ability**.

capable: see **able**.

capacity: see **ability**.

cardinal: see **ordinal**.

carefree, careless Both imply lack of care but their meanings are quite distinct:
   carefree: without any worries or responsibilities (or sense of responsibility).
   careless: without enough care, thought or attention.
   It follows that a carefree person is not necessarily careless.

carousal, carousel
   carousal: noisy drinking-spree.
   carousel: merry-go-round; rotating conveyor (e.g. for luggage at airport) or holder (e.g. for film-slides in projector).
   The first rhymes with *arousal*. The second is pronounced *cara-sell*, with the stress on the final syllable.

cast, caste Pronounced alike. *Caste* means *social class, system or position*

31

castor, caster

(notably in Hindu society, but also generally on the basis of birth, wealth, religion, trade, etc.). In all other cases, *cast* is required.

castor, caster   Variants of the same word. Either spelling is acceptable for the finely-ground sugar (usually *caster*), the swivelled wheel on furniture, etc. (usually *castor*) and the container with a perforated lid for sprinkling flour, sugar, etc. (usually *caster*). *Castor* is invariable in *castor oil*.

Catholic, catholic   The meaning is *universal*. A capital letter is used in religious contexts: *Roman Catholic, Anglo-Catholic, a Catholic*. With a small letter, the word is usually found in such phrases as *catholic tastes*, where the meaning is *liberal, wide-ranging*.

Celsius, centigrade   *Celsius* has become familiar since its adoption by weather forecasters. It means the same as *centigrade* which is a scale of temperature measurement having a hundred degrees, the freezing-point of water being zero and the boiling-point 100 degrees. *Celsius* is the name of the man who invented the scale.

Celtic, Gaelic, Gallic

> *Celtic*: having to do with the Celts (roughly, the Highland Scottish, Irish, Welsh, Manx, Cornish and Breton people); the language of these. (Pronounced with initial *K*.)
>
> *Gaelic*: having to do with, mainly, the Scottish Celts; the language of these.
>
> *Gallic*: having to do with the Gauls. Loosely, French (*Gallic wit/charm*, etc.).

censor, censure

> *censor* (verb):   suppress or edit on grounds of morals, obscenity, national security, etc. Also noun: person who does this. Also *censorship*, act of doing this.
>
> *censure* (verb):   criticise harshly; deliver reprimand. Also noun: act of doing this (*vote of censure*).

The corresponding adjectives are *censorial* and *censorious*.

census: see **consensus**.

centenary, centennial

> *centenary*:   hundredth anniversary.
>
> *centennial*:   lasting a hundred years or occurring every hundred years.

centigrade: see **Celsius**.

centipede, millipede Commonly thought to indicate insects with a hundred or a thousand legs respectively. Not so. There are thousands of species, and the number of legs ranges from a few dozen to several hundred. The two words merely indicate two main classes of insects with lots of legs.

ceremonial, ceremonious
> *ceremonial*: with ceremony; formal (*a ceremonial occasion*). Also noun: rite or formality, or its observation.
> *ceremonious*: addicted to ceremony; punctilious; pompous; self-important. Often *unceremoniously*, without standing on ceremony; hurriedly and without dignity or politeness.

chandelier: see **candelabrum**.

chaotic: see **inchoate**.

chart, charter As verbs:
> *chart*: to map.
> *charter*: to hire.

A *chartered* yacht may sail *uncharted* (not *unchartered*) waters.

chary, wary Both mean *cautious*. *Chary* (related to the word *care*) has the sense of being careful, shy or sparing, even mean, in one's actions. *Wary* (related to *beware*) carries the sense of being watchful, guarded or suspicious in inclination.

The corresponding adverbs are the uncommon *charily* and the familiar *warily* (as in *tread warily*).

chastise, chasten The primary meaning of *chastise* is *punish by thrashing* but the normal meaning is *scold or criticise severely*. To *chasten* is to correct or subdue by the infliction of suffering or punishment. A person who is *chastened* is subdued and improved by an experience from which he has learnt a lesson.

check, cheque The first is the American spelling of the second.

cherish: see **nurture**.

childlike, childish Both mean *in the manner of a child*, but the first is complimentary (*innocent, trusting*, etc.) and the second is derogatory

chord, cord

(*immature, foolish* etc.). The words are normally applied to adults. They stress, respectively, the appealing and less appealing characteristics of children.

chord, cord   *Cord* is the word for rope or string, *chord* for all other meanings, including the musical *chord* (which may be played on strings) and the figurative *strike a chord* (evoke a memory).

circumvent, circumnavigate

circumvent: get round, avoid, find a way round (*circumvent a problem*).

circumnavigate: sail round (*circumnavigate the world*).

The second is sometimes mistakenly used in the place of the first.

cite: see **quote**.

citizen, denizen   Both are inhabitants but a *denizen* is particularly a foreigner who has become resident, a plant or animal adopted from elsewhere, or a naturalised word.

civic, civil, civilian

civic: relating to a city or town (or citizens or citizenship). *Civic duty/centre/function* have to do with the local community, which is the special emphasis in *civic*.

civil: relating to a citizen as an individual; distinguished from matters that are legal (*civil rights/liberty* are those not guaranteed by law), military (*civil war* is between people, not armies fighting on behalf of countries), or religious (*civil wedding*). *Civil* has to do with the individual in society.

civilian: relating to the citizen as distinct from military personnel: *Civilian employees on an army base/The Merchant Navy is a civilian service*. Non-military planes are customarily *civil* aircraft, however.

classic, classical, classics   The basic distinction is between:

classic: of the highest quality (*a classic performance*); perfectly typical (*a classic case of mistaken identity*).

classical: pertaining to or characteristic of the civilisation and culture of ancient Greek or Rome.

Strictly speaking, *classical music/architecture/ballet* is that which has the formality, restraint and balance associated with *classical* art, so that to describe music or architecture as *classical* is merely to differentiate it from music or architecture belonging to another style or period, such as the more florid baroque. In practice *classical* has come to mean *belonging to any period of excellence* (so that *classical music* is differentiated from popular music), and *classical* begins to blur with *classic*. This must be defined as loose.

Classics, however, legitimately brings the two together. The classics are things of the highest quality (*modern classics*) and the literature of Greece and Rome.

clean, cleanse Originally restricted to moral, spiritual or ritual purification, *cleanse* has come to mean no more than *clean* (as a verb) though it is limited to the physical removal of dirt (*cleansing powder* for the sink, *cleansing-cream* for face and hands, the *cleansing department* of the local council). It cannot be used as a general substitute for *clean* as a verb (in *clean out, clean up*, etc.) or adjective (*clean break*, etc.).

cleanliness, cleanness *Cleanliness* relates to *cleanly* (habitually clean) and *cleanness* to **clean**, but this distinction is generally lost. Either will do for *freedom from grime* but only *cleanness* can be used of lines/driving licence/limbs/shape/cut/living, etc.

cleanse: see **clean**.

clench, clinch Formerly interchangeable, these verbs are now distinct.
  clench: close (fist, teeth, etc.) firmly.
  clinch: settle (argument, deal) decisively.
A *clinch* is, informally, an embrace, including one in boxing.

client, customer Snobbery dictates that a professional person (whatever that means nowadays) has a *client* but a mere shopkeeper has a *customer*. This honourable word does not deserve to be regarded as an inferior one. The sooner the distinction is dropped the better.

climatic, climactic, climacteric
  climatic: having to do with climate.
  climactic: having to do with a climax.
  Climacteric is a rarer word. As a noun it signifies a crucial event or period; it also exists as an adjective. It can also mean the same as *menopause*.

cloth, clothe *Cloth* is the noun, now usually restricted to a piece of material used for cleaning, and *clothe* the verb meaning to *dress* or *cover*. *Clothes* is the general noun for garments.

Cloth rhymes with *moth* and *clothe(s)* with *loathe(s)*.

clue, cue, queue   Both a *clue* and a *cue* are signs; the former is one that points towards the solution of a problem or mystery, and the latter is one that prompts a person to act or speak.

A *cue* is also a rod used in billiards. A *queue* is a line of waiting people, cars, etc.

coarse, course   *Coarse* is the adjective (*rough*), *course* the noun or verb with many meanings.

cohere: see **adhere, cohesion** and **cohesive**.

cohesion, coherence   The distinction is the same as that in **cohesive, coherent**, to which these two nouns correspond. The first occurs most frequently in physical, the second in abstract contexts.

  cohesion: sticking or working together (*the cohesion of a team*).
  coherence: consistency, natural connection (*the coherence of the policy*).
See **cohesive**.

cohesive, coherent   The verb *cohere* (stick together) gives both of these adjectives, the first of which is normally used of people or physical things, the second of abstractions.

  cohesive: staying together (*a cohesive fighting force; a cohesive family*).
  coherent: connected, consistent in thought, so as to be understood (*a coherent speech/argument/explanation*).
See **cohesion**.

coiffeur, coiffure   Fancy words for hairdresser and hairstyle respectively. French always sounds grander than English. (The opposite is true in France!)

collaborate: see **cooperate**.

collate, collect   To *collate* is to examine (a number of things, such as facts or notes) in order to compare them and put them in order. The word is especially used of organising, checking or correcting the order of pages in a document. The police *collate* evidence to discern patterns of agreement and disagreement. They may *collect* it too, but that is a different process.

collusion, cooperation Both mean *working together or agreeing*, but *collusion* is always for an improper purpose. *Cooperation* has no such colouring.

combat, contest Both are struggles but a *combat* is always a fight whereas a *contest* may be merely a competition, even a good-natured one.

comic, comical
> *comic*: intending (whether successful or not) to cause comedy (*a comic actor*).
> *comical*: causing laughter (whether intended or not).

A *comic* performance may fail to raise a smile, whereas a tragic performance may be highly *comical*.

Only *comic* is also a noun, denoting a comedian, a comic magazine or (informally and ironically) an incomptent person. As an informal adjective it means *incompetent*.

commissionaire, commissioner A *commissionaire* is a uniformed doorkeeper, usually at a hotel, and a *commissioner* is a person given powers (i.e. a *commission*) to do stated work. The Parliamentary Commissioner, for example, is appointed to investigate citizens' complaints against government.

commitment, committal Though these have exactly the same meaning (the act of committing – entrusting, consigning, pledging, performing, etc. – or the state of being committed), in practice they are not interchangeable. *Committal* is a formal word, seldom found outside legal contexts (*committal proceedings/to prison/of a crime* – though most people would speak of the *committing* of a crime) and religious services (*committal of a body to the grave/cremation/the sea*). The normal word is *commitment*, usually in the sense of committing oneself, as an obligation, promise or act of loyalty, to a cause or course of action (*sense of commitment to one's job; financial commitments*). It often means no more than *personal devotion*, *directed energy* or *granting* (of money, etc.).

common: see **mutual**.

compact, contract The meaning is *agreement, bargain*, but a *contract* is a formal, legally binding one whereas a *compact* is merely mutual (and may be made for illegal purposes).

comparable, incomparable Even though these look like, and in fact are, opposites, they are not used as such. *Comparable* means *able or*

comparative, comparable

worthy to be compared, usually in the sense of *similar*. The normal opposite is *not comparable*. *Incomparable* means *without equal (an incomparable view from the summit)*.

Both words are pronounced with the stress on the *com-*, not the *-ar-*. See **compare** and **comparative**.

comparative, comparable
Comparative means *involving comparison, relative*. If an attempt, say, is a *comparative failure* it is not an absolute failure but a failure when compared with something else, such as what was hoped for or what happened on a previous attempt.

Comparable means *able or worthy to be compared*, usually in the sense of *similar*.

See **compare** and **comparable**.

compare, contrast

compare:	set together to observe agreement and disagreement (*Compare notes*).
compare to:	note similarities; liken (*His management style has been compared to Atilla the Hun's*).
compare with:	note similarities and differences (*She does not like to be compared with her brother*).

Without an object, *compare* means *bear comparison* or *rival* and is followed by *with*: *This house cannot compare/compares badly with the other.*

contrast:	note differences by comparison (*The latest opinion poll contrasts with last month's*).

See **comparative**.

compel, impel Both mean *force into action* but *compel* is the stronger, suggesting the application of external force over which one has no control. *Impel* implies that the force comes from within oneself, and can also mean merely *urge, incite or motivate towards action* without such action necessarily happening. But *compel* has the sense of *obligation* to act.

compelling: see **compulsory**.

compile, compose One *compiles* a list, report, dictionary, crossword or score, but *composes* a letter or piece of music. A team may be *composed* of eleven players. Both words mean *put together*, but in *compile* the emphasis is on collecting piecemeal or from a number of sources, whereas in *compose* it is on the unified form of the finished work.

For **compose** see also **comprise**.

complacent, complaisant, compliant

> *complacent*: smug, self-satisfied.
> *complaisant*: wishing to please; acquiescing in order to please.
> *compliant*: obedient, yielding.

Compliant shares some of the sense of *complaisant* (which is not much used) but the emphasis is different, being on submission or submissiveness without necessarily any desire to please.

complement, compliment, supplement   The first two, and the first and last, are often confused.

> *complement*: that which makes something complete. (A bus with a full *complement* has the maximum number of passengers.)
> *compliment*: expression of regard or praise.
> *supplement*: that which is added, as an extra part, to something already complete. (Payment for a part-time job is a *supplement* to one's normal income.)

All three may be used as verbs with these senses.

complementary, complimentary, supplementary   The adjectives correspond to **complement, compliment, supplement** (see entry above) and the same distinctions apply. *Complimentary*, in the expression *complimentary tickets*, usually mean no more than *free*, though the strict sense is *given as a sign of respect*.

completeness, completion

> *completeness*: the state of being complete.
> *completion*: the act of making complete.

Thus the *completeness* of a book is the thoroughness with which it covers its subject (though *complete* can mean *accomplished* in the sense of *consummate*, in which case *completeness* can mean *accomplishment*). The *completion* of a book is the act of finishing it.

compliant: see **complacent**.

compliment: see **complement**.

comportment, deportment   A person's *deportment* is his behaviour, demeanour or manners, especially when they are cultivated; the word is specifically applied to physical bearing and posture, though in American English it has more to do with general conduct. *Comportment* – a new word which not all dictionaries allow – is fitting behaviour or behaviour of a specified kind: *comport with* means *suit, befit, agree (with)*.

comprehensible, comprehensive The verb *comprehend* offers two meanings: *understand* and *include, comprise*. *Comprehensible* (understandable) is the adjective corresponding to the first, *comprehensive* (all-inclusive) to the second.

See **apprehend** and **comprise**.

comprise, compose, constitute *Compose* and *constitute* both mean *form, make up*. *Compose* means *form by putting together* (*Five ingredients are needed to compose the salad*) and is usually used in the passive (*The salad is composed of . . .*). *Constitute* need not include the idea of *putting together* and is usually active: *The lack of ventilation constitutes a health hazard.*

Comprise means *contain, include, consist of*. Whereas *compose/constitute* mean *form*, *comprise* means *be formed of* (or *be composed of* or even *be constituted of*). It is a converse of the other two. We may say *The Library comprises a million volumes* or *A million volumes constitute/compose the Library* but not *. . . comprise the Library.*

Comprise normally has a plural object. The other two normally have a plural subject.

For **compose** see also **compile**.

For **comprise** see also **consist of**.

compulsory, compulsive, compelling, impulsive
 compulsory: obligatory.
 compulsive: acting under compulsion; having an uncontrollable urge (*a compulsive drinker*).
 compelling: forcing one's interest.
 impulsive: acting by sudden whim; rash, hasty.

Compulsive and *compelling* overlap in meaning *having the power to compel*. A television series may be *compulsive/compelling* viewing, the first implying that viewers are likely to become addicted, the second that the programme commands attention.

concave, convex
 concave: curved like the inner surface of a hollow sphere.
 convex: curved like the outer surface of a hollow sphere.

conciliation: see **reconciliation**.

conclave, enclave
 conclave: private assembly for discussion.
 enclave: territory or culturally distinct unit enclosed by foreign territory or different culture.

The meeting of cardinals to elect a new pope is also called a *conclave*.

condole, console
> *condole*: express sympathy. Always followed by *with*.
> *console*: comfort. Always followed by direct object.

confident, confidant *Confident* is the adjective, *confidant* an uncommon noun meaning *person one confides in*. If the person is feminine the word may be spelt *confidante*; in either case it is pronounced with the stress on the final syllable, which is *ant* irrespective of gender.

confound, confuse Both have the meaning (among others) of *bewilder*, but it is normally a person who is *confounded* whereas both people and things may be *confused*.

congenial, congenital So far apart in meaning that using one for the other must be regarded as malapropism rather than legitimate confusion.
> *congenial*: agreeable; to one's taste; of the same tastes.
> *congenital*: (of diseases) dating from birth.

conjugal, connubial Neither is much used. Both mean *having to do with marriage*, but usage dictates that *conjugal* appertains to the rights of man and wife (*conjugal home, conjugal rights*) and *connubial* to the marriage-service (*connubial vows*) and the state of marriage generally (*connubial bliss*).

connive, conspire Both have the sense of *plot together to do wrong*. *Conspire* is the stronger word, *connive* suggesting less serious wrongdoing. *Connive* has the additional meaning of *tolerate or ignore something* (usually wrongdoing), thus encouraging it.

connote, denote A word is said to *connote* something if it suggests or implies secondary meanings/associations/emotions additional to (or other than) its primary or literal meaning. A word is said to *denote* something if it indicates, signifies or, simply, means it. The word *family* denotes the people we live with; for some it connotes (or has *connotations* of) love and security, though for others it may connote lovelessness and poverty. Sunrise denotes the beginning of a new day and may connote fresh hope.

> To use *connote* for *denote* is a common looseness: to use *denote* for *connote* is plain wrong.

connubial: see **conjugal**.

consecutive, successive These share the sense *following on one after the*

41

other in a series but *consecutive* has the refinement, not shared by *successive*, of implying a regular order, e.g. logical, numerical, chronological, etc. Hence *five consecutive days of sunshine* (five out of five) but *five successive attempts to reach the summit* (at intervals, not necessarily regular ones).

consensus, census   Nothing in the meaning of these words should give rise to any confusion.

> *consensus*: agreement of opinion.
>
> *census*:   (official) count (e.g. of traffic, population).

In view of the definition of *consensus* the italicised words in the frequently encountered 'the *general* consensus *of opinion*' are tautological.

consent: see **assent**.

consequent, subsequent, consequential   The major distinction is between *consequent* (*on*) (*following as a result or logical conclusion*) and *subsequent* (*to*) (*following in time*). The notion of cause and effect must be present if *consequent* is to be used. Hence *the fog and the consequent accidents* but *the fog and the subsequent sunshine*.

Although *consequential* can mean the same as *consequent*, it seldom is used in this sense. It is nearly always found in legal or commercial contexts meaning *following as an indirect result* (as in *consequential damages* which may be, for example, the costs of flying home after an accident abroad, the accident having necessitated but not caused the flight). More usually it means *self-important*, and more frequently still it is found in the negative form *inconsequential*, meaning *trivial*.

See **inconsequential**.

conserve, preserve   Overlap is evident in *conserve* (*keep entire, retain*) and *preserve* (*keep from harm or loss*) and the difference is mainly one of usage rather than meaning: one tends to *conserve* energy, land, rivers and forests, but *preserve* fruit, old buildings and wild life. Whether jam is a *conserve* or *preserve* is a matter of choice; if anything, a *conserve* is more likely to contain whole pieces of fruit. But only a person can be *well-preserved*.

consist of, comprise, consist in   Meaning *be made up of*, the first two are interchangeable: *The furniture in the room consists of/comprises a bed and a wardrobe.* A common mistake is to say *comprises of* or *is comprised of*. Never use *of* after *comprise*.

Consist in means *be defined as* or *have as its essential or main feature*. It is usually followed by an abstraction: *Success in this job consists in good public relations*.

See also **comprise**.

consistent, persistent   The idea of repetition underlies both of these words.

   consistent: constant, fixed; showing conformity with previous practice.

   persistent: continuing obstinately; continuing to exist.

There are positive connotations in the first, negative ones in the second: *consistent sunshine/persistent rain, consistent punctuality/persistent lateness, consistent health/persistent illness*. More precisely, *persistent* suggests repetition that is deliberate, or perverse, or in troublesome circumstances; *consistent* merely implies repetition in the same fashion: *persistent questions/consistent excellence*.

console: see **condole**.

consortium, consortia   *Consortium*, a fancy word for a group of bodies acting in combination (e.g. a number of companies getting together to bid for a contract), is singular. Its plural is *consortia*. Such uses as *a consortia* and *the consortia is* . . . . are therefore solecisms.

conspire: see **connive**.

constant: see **continual**.

constraint, restraint   Both denote force preventing one from doing something.

   restraint: the ability to hold back (or the act of holding back or being held back) from some action.

   constraint: something that prevents one from doing something.

The normal distinction is that *restraint* is a restriction people exercise to control themselves (*He showed exceptional restraint under provocation*) or others (*Use physical restraint*). *Constraint* is a restriction imposed from without, especially by circumstances: financial shortages or social conventions, for example, may place *constraints* on people's freedom.

contagious, infectious   These words are used of diseases:

   contagious: spread by direct contact with diseased person.

   infectious: spread by micro-organisms (in air, water, etc.).

   Figuratively, they are interchangeable: *contagious enthusiasm, infectious laughter*.

contemporary, contemporaneous, modern

contemporary:	of the same period (*Florence Nightingale was contemporary with Queen Victoria*).
contemporaneous:	existing or occurring during the same time (*The buildings are contemporaneous*).
modern:	of the present time.

The problem with *contemporary* is that it has come to mean the same as *modern* (e.g. *contemporary furniture*). Though loose, and unnecessary, this has to be accepted as usage, though it does give rise to ambiguity. *We live in an eighteenth century cottage with contemporary furniture* should mean that the furniture is eighteenth century. If it is twentieth century, use *modern*.

Contemporary and *contemporaneous* mean the same (except that *contemporary* can be used as a noun: *We were contemporaries at school*), but as adjectives *contemporary* is normally used of people, *contemporaneous* of things or abstractions.

contemptible, contemptuous

contemptible:	deserving contempt
contemptuous:	showing contempt.

Contemptible behaviour is despicable; *contemptuous behaviour* is scornful or arrogant.

contents, content   *Contents* are whatever is in a container (*contents of a bottle/parcel/drawer*) or contained in anything else (*contents of a house/mixture/newspaper*). The *contents of a book* are its chapters.

Content means *kind of contents*: the content of an argument/letter/report is its meaning or substance. The content of a book is its subject-matter.

contest: see **combat**.

contiguous: see **adjacent**.

continual, continuous, constant

continual:	continuing but with interruptions (*continual storms/complaints/questions*).
continuous:	continuing without interruption (*continuous rain/noise/discomfort*).
constant:	continuing without change (with or without interruption).

In certain contexts the three are interchangeable. A struggle against poverty, for example, may be described as continual, continuous or constant, the point being that it is *continuing*, and that the word *struggle* itself implies *continual* ups and downs within a *continuous* process. In general, however, careful writers discriminate between *continual* and *continuous*, or use *constant* (which will do for either) if they are in doubt.

continuance, continuation, continuity   An act or fact of continuing can be both a *continuance* and a *continuation*. The first additionally suggests carrying on without stopping (*She was bored by the continuance of the quarrel*) or duration. The second additionally implies carrying on after a break (*the continuation of a journey*) or as a sequel. *Continuity* is the state of being uninterrupted or in orderly sequence (*His re-election guarantees continuity of policy*): it is related to **continuous** (see **continual**).

contract: see **compact**.

contrary, converse, inverse   As adjectives, the first two words mean *opposite*. *Inverse* means *opposite in effect, sequence or tendency* or, if you like, *reversed* (back to front, upside down, etc.). It is customary for three prize-winners in a competition to be announced in *inverse order*, the third first, etc.

contrast: see **compare**.

converse: see **contrary**.

convex: see **concave**.

cooperate, collaborate   Often used as synonyms, meaning *work together*, but there is a slight difference of emphasis. *Collaborate* is preferable when there is close association on a specific project (*collaborate in the preparation of a report*) or when the context is sinister (*collaborate with the enemy/in a crime*). *Cooperate* would not be wrong, only faintly unidiomatic, in such cases. It is the more all–purpose word, capable too of a general sense of *act in an understanding manner* (*Everyone cooperated during the emergency*: *collaborate* would sound a little odd here).

   Cooperate may be hyphened (*co-operate*), as many prefer, because this seems a natural way of separating two o's differently pronounced. The word is so familiar, though, that few people are likely to need such a guide to pronunciation, and it is common for hyphens to fall away unless they perform an essential function.

cooperation: see **collusion**.

copious: see **fulsome**.

cord: see **chord**.

core: see **corps**.

corporal, corporeal   *Corporal*, meaning *of the human body*, is not much found outside the expression *corporal punishment*. *Corporeal*, meaning *having a human body*, is mainly encountered in religious contexts in its general sense of *material* (as opposed to *spiritual*).

corps, core, corpse, corpus   The most likely confusion is between *corps* and *core*, both of which rhyme with *tore*. A *corps* is a group of people, but by custom and habit the word is restricted to a few very specific groups (the *diplomatic corps*, for example), usually in military circles (*army cadet corps*) but also in ballet, where the *corps de ballet* comprises the dancers who perform as a group, not as soloists. A *core* is a central part.

A *corpse* is a dead body, and a *corpus* a collection of writings, usually by one author or by several on one topic.

correspond with, correspond to
> *correspond with*: exchange letters with.
>
> *correspond to*:   be in agreement with or similar to (*wage increases that correspond to cost-of-living increases*).

With is common with this second sense (especially when the meaning is *in agreement with*) though *to* remains more natural when the meaning is *similar to*. In either case, *with* is acceptable.

To, however, is never possible in the first sense.

correspondingly: see **similarly**.

corroborate: see **verify**.

corrosion, erosion   What these have in common is *gradual deterioration*, but *corrosion* is by eating away, often by chemical action, as in the *corrosion* of a car's bodywork by rust, whereas *erosion* is by wearing away, as the *erosion* of cliffs by the action of the sea.

cosmonaut: see **astronaut**.

council(lor), counsel(lor)
> *council*:   group of people elected or appointed to govern, administer, advise, discuss, etc.
>
> *counsel*:   advice, guidance, opinion, discussion. Also a barrister. (Also verb.)

Hence a *councillor* (member of a council) and a *counsellor* (person who offers counsel, e.g. a marriage-guidance counsellor).

course: see **coarse**.

courtesy, curtsy   Related by derivation and meaning, the first means *politeness*, the second being the gesture of respect made by women bending their knees in greeting to royalty. The spelling *curtsey* is also possible.

crass, gross   Interchangeable in the sense of **flagrant** (*crass stupidity, gross ignorance*). *Crass* also means *extremely stupid* (*crass behaviour*) and *gross* also means *repulsively fat, coarse* (in behaviour), *total* (*gross amount*) and *thick*.

credence, credibility, credulity

credence: belief, acceptance (*No-one gives much credence to his claims*).

credibility: quality of being worthy of belief *(story lacks credibility)*; quality of being able to convince *(lacks credibility as a candidate for promotion)*.

credulity: quality of being ready to believe something on little or no evidence; gullibility (*showed credulity in buying it from a total stranger*).

There is often confusion between the first two. *Credence* is something one gives or shows; *credibility* is a quality somebody or something has.

See **credible**.

credible, creditable, credulous

credible: believable, reliable (*a credible witness*); convincing (*a credible reputation*).

creditable: deserving commendation (*a creditable result*).

credulous: gullible *(voters so credulous that they believed him)*.

The opposites are *incredible* (unbelievable), *discreditable* (dishonourable) and *incredulous* (disbelieving).

See **credence**.

crevasse, crevice

crevasse: deep cleft in glacier.

crevice: narrow crack, small fissure (in rock, wall, ice, ground, etc.).

The first has the accent on the final syllable, the second on the first syllable.

criterion, criteria *Criterion* is the singular, *criteria* the plural. It is a common error to assume that *criteria* is a singular noun. It is wrong to say *a criteria, the criteria is,* etc.

The plural form *criterions* is acceptable (in the way that foreign words often develop the English plural -s instead of their original foreign plural form), but is so unusual as to invite suspicions of ignorance. *Criterias,* however, is nonsensical.

crotch, crutch Little to choose here. Tailors seem to prefer *crotch* for that part of trousers where the inside legs join, but *crutch* will do as well. *Crutch* is probably the more common word for the fork of the human body and the adjacent genital area, and the only word for the prop used by a person with his leg in plaster.

crumble, crumple
> *crumble*: break or fall into pieces (like crumbs). Also figurative: *his hopes crumbled* (disintegrated).
> *crumple*: crush or become crushed into folds or wrinkles (*a crumpled suit*); collapse (*She crumpled into tears*)

The first of these definitions of *crumple* is the same as one of the definitions of **rumple.** The second is not.

See **rumble.**

crutch: see **crotch.**

cudgel, bludgeon These are weapons in the form of a stick or club. Both words also function as verbs meaning *beat with a cudgel/bludgeon.* Figuratively, *cudgel* is usually found in *cudgel one's brains* (think hard) and *take up the cudgels* (join in defence). *Bludgeon* is more general, often as a verb meaning *argue with brutal force.*

cue: see **clue.**

cultivated, cultured Generally interchangeable in the sense of *refined, well-educated, showing good taste. Cultured* is the slightly broader word, expressing wide-ranging artistic and social graces. *Cultivated* is more appropriate when a person has particular ones.

curb, kerb In British English a *kerb* is the edge between a pavement and a road; *curb* is a noun meaning *anything that restrains* and a verb meaning *restrain* (*should curb his tendency to shout*). American English uses *curb* for all of these.

currant, current *Currant* is the fruit. Use *current* in all other senses.

curricula, curricular *Curricula* is the plural of *curriculum*, of which *curricular* is the adjectival form (*Some schools are resistant to curricular change*).

The plural *curriculums* is acceptable: see note on **criterion**.

curtsy: see **courtesy**.

customer: see **client**.

cynical, sceptical
> *cynical*: disinclined to believe.
> *sceptical*: inclined to disbelieve.

These definitions highlight the negative nature of *cynical*: it implies a morose cast of mind which is habitually distrustful of people's motives, especially of human benevolence. *Sceptical* usually means little more than *doubtful*: it is applied to a specific withholding of belief on certain occasions rather than a characteristic pessimism.

See **sceptic**.

D

dappled, piebald Usually applied to animals, especially horses.
> *dappled*: marked with spots.
> *piebald*: black and white in patches.

data, datum The struggle to preserve *data* as the plural form of *datum* has probably been lost as a result of the advent of computers, which has meant that such expressions as *this data* (for *these data*) and *the data is* (for *are*) have swamped correct usage. *Data* has now virtually replaced the singular noun *information* in computer jargon, and is here to stay as a singular itself. But it properly refers to a number of observations, measurements or facts, any one of which is a *datum*, and good scientists still observe the difference.

Data-bank or *data processing* are, however, singular terms in which *data* has an adjectival function.

dazed, dazzled To be *dazed* is to be stunned, stupefied or bewildered by a blow to the head or, figuratively, as if by such a blow (e.g. on hearing bad news). To be *dazzled* is to be blinded by strong light shining into the eyes or, figuratively, amazed by any brilliant display (e.g. of expertise).

deadly, deathly

> *deadly*: causing or threatening death (*deadly sin, deadly enemy*); very boring (*The function was deadly*); extremely (*deadly dull*); very great (*in deadly earnest*).
>
> *deathly*: like death (*deathly silence*).

debar, disbar   It is a mistake to use the second for the first, but people quite frequently do so, perhaps because it seems natural to reach for a *dis-* word to express a negative idea (*disagree, disbelief, discontinue*, etc.).

> *debar*: exclude (*debarred from membership because of his age*).
>
> *disbar*: (of barristers only) expel from practice.

decease, disease

> *decease*: death.
>
> *disease*: cause of sickness.

In the first, *-cease* is pronounced *cease*; in the second, both s's are pronounced as z's.

deceit, deception   Both mean *act of deceiving*, but additionally:

> *deceit*:   anything intended to deceive; fraud.
>
> *deception*: state of being deceived; means of deceiving; trick.

Both imply deliberate dishonesty. *Deceit* stresses the intention to deceive, *deception* the successful accomplishment. *Deception* can also denote innocuous illusion (*a conjuror's deception*).

Generally *deceit* implies the habit of dishonesty, *deception* the individual act.

See **deceitful**.

deceitful, deceptive   The first is the stronger (and more condemnatory) word, implying dishonesty and the deliberate intention to deceive. In contrast, *deceptive* may be used to imply no intentional deception: a person's *deceptive appearance* may, for example, be down-at-heel whereas he is in fact wealthy.

> *deceitful*:   full of deceit, wishing to deceive.
>
> *deceptive*:   likely to deceive; misleading.

For the corresponding nouns see **deceit, deception**.

In general terms, people are *deceitful* and things are *deceptive*.

decided, decisive

> *decided*: unmistakable (*walk with a decided limp*).
>
> *decisive*: conclusive (*decisive battle*); deciding (*decisive lead*, one that is likely to determine the outcome); showing power of decision (*decisive leader*).

decimate, defeat   Those who know some Latin point out that the prefix *deci-* denotes a tenth (as in *decimal*, etc.) and that *decimate* means *kill one in ten* as the Romans did to control mutinous elements in their armies. Be that as it may, the word is usually used to mean *defeat* or *reduce heavily*, *dismember* or *kill most of*. As such it is here to stay, though the loose senses will be avoided by careful users of the language.

decry, descry   Originally related, but now quite distinct.
>   *decry*:   condemn; disparage (*must not decry their attempts to solve the problem*).
>   *descry*: catch sight of.

The second is rare and rather high-flown.

deduce, deduct: see **adduce**.

deduction: see **induction**.

defeat: see **decimate**.

defective, deficient   Sometimes thought to mean the same because they both denote that something is wrong and imply a cause for complaint, but they are in fact separate.
>   *defective*: having a defect or fault.
>   *deficient*: having a deficiency or lack: incomplete, inadequate.

There are occasions when the second is used to mean *lacking in quality* and the first would be equally appropriate, but usually there is a clear case for one or the other.

defensible, defensive
>   *defensible*: able to be defended (*a defensible policy* is a justifiable one). Opposite: *indefensible*.
>   *defensive*:   acting in defence (*defensive football* concentrates on defence rather than attack; a *defensive answer* is worded without aggression and with the intention of fending off criticism). Opposite: *aggressive*.

deficient: see **defective**.

definite, definitive   The second is not a fancier variant of the first. The meanings should be carefully distinguished.
>   *definite*:   clear, unambiguous; sure; defining precisely.
>   *definitive*: conclusive (*a definitive victory*); most authoritative, so as not to be superseded (*a definitive history book*).

A *definite* answer is precise; a *definitive* one is unchallengeable.
Definitive is pronounced with the stress on the second syllable.

delegate, relegate As verbs:
> *delegate*: give (responsibility, power, duty) to someone as one's representative.
>
> *relegate*: place (person or thing) in a lower, less prominent position (*relegate the matter to the back of one's mind*).

delimit: see **limit**.

delusion: for **delusion/illusion**, see **allusion**.

demonic, demoniacal Someone's glee or energy or laughter may be *demonic* (like a demon; fiendish) or *demoniacal* (as if possessed by a demon; frenzied). It probably matters little if the intention is to communicate a sense of unnatural or immoderate destructiveness or ferocity of the kind associated with evil spirits. But the words have different overtones. *Demonic* is harmless hyperbole, often tinged with admiration. *Demoniacal*, with its suggestion of possession, hints at lack of mental or emotional balance.

demur, demure An occasional pronunciation problem for some who want to say 'I must *demur*' (register disagreement) but who find themselves saying *demure* (reserved, modest).

The first, a verb, is pronounced with the *-ur* as in *recur*. The second, an adjective, has the *-ure* as in *sure*. In both, the stress is on the last syllable.

denizen: see **citizen**.

denote: see **connote**.

deny: see **refute**.

dependability: see **dependency**.

dependant, dependent The first is used only as the word for *a person* who depends on someone for support, usually financial. In all other cases *dependent* is needed (*dependent relative; dependent on her agreement*).

dependency, dependence, dependability A *dependency* is a thing that is dependent on something else; it is usually a country that is subordinate to the control of another though not formally part of it.

It is wrong to use the word as a variant of *dependence*, which means *the state of being dependent* (e.g. dependence on a drug). It also means *trust, confidence, reliance* (e.g. dependence on a person).

Dependability is reliability.

deportation: see **transport**.

deportment: see **comportment**.

depositary, depository, repository   The first (sometimes spelt like the second) is a little-used word for a person to whom something is entrusted. A *depository* is a storehouse where something is deposited (e.g. furniture for storage in safekeeping). *Repository* can mean the same, though it usually denotes a smaller storage place. More frequently, however, it is a person or thing acting as a store of something non-physical, such as information, wisdom, knowledge or secrets: a dictionary could be described as a respository. So could a place of storage and exhibition: *museum which is the finest respository of Elizabethan miniatures.* The word has other meanings (a **confidant**, a burial place) but these are less common.

deprecate, depreciate   *Deprecate* means *express disapproval or disapprove of* as in *He deprecates physical violence. Depreciate* is usually used to mean *reduce or diminish in value or price (A car depreciates rapidly).* Its less common meaning (*disparage, belittle*) approaches that of *deprecate,* with resultant misuse. There is a difference between *express disapproval* (*deprecate*) and *express contempt* (*depreciate*) and it should be observed.

deprivation, privation, depredation   *Deprivation* is the state of having something (usually desirable) taken away. The sense of *loss* is central. The word is commonly, but wrongly, used in such expressions as *social deprivation.* This means, strictly speaking, that certain people have lost certain advantages in life. The truth, usually, is that they never had them in the first place. What is needed, therefore, is *insufficiency* or *inadequacy,* but *deprivation* has the advantage of implying that people are being deliberately victimised by having something taken away, i.e. a political or sociological point is being made.

   Privation is quite different: it means *lack of the basic necessities of life.*

   Depredation is plundering, preying upon, robbery, ravages, etc. (*the depredations of the storm*).

derisive, derisory
>   *derisive*: showing contempt (*derisive laughter*).
>   *derisory*: deserving contempt (*derisory wage increase*).

descry: see **decry**.

desert, dessert   *Dessert* is what you eat at or towards the end of a meal.

despatch

Desert is needed in all other cases, whether the accent is on the first syllable (*a desolate region*) or the second (*quit*).

The plural noun *deserts* means *what is deserved* (as in *got his just deserts*). Pronounced exactly like *desserts*, this may be a source of comic confusion.

despatch: see **dispatch**.

despoil: see **spoil**.

destined, predestined, predetermined *Destined* means *having a destination* (*an aircraft destined for Rome*) and *intended* (designed, appointed, meant, designated, etc.) *in advance* (*a young player destined to become better known as a coach*). Generally it is used to mean *known later* (*It was not destined to succeed* = *It failed, as is now known*) or *foreordained*.

This last meaning is close to that *predestined* (*determined beforehand*) which has two emphases. First, it is often used of something that inevitably fails, the sense being *fated*; second, it is used to indicate divine intention or destiny. *Predetermine* also means *determine* (or plan) *in advance* but implies human rather than divine intention.

detract, distract

    detract (*from*): diminish, take away (usually something good) (from).

    distract: turn (the mind) aside (e.g. by confusing, amusing, troubling, etc.).

Sometimes used interchangeably: in *His failure detracts from his high reputation* it might be possible to use *distracts from* in the sense of *diverts people's attention away from*, but this might sound like a mistake. The two words are generally distinct.

deviant, devious The two are related to *deviate* (differ, turn aside).

    deviant: deviating from what is acceptable or normal.

    devious: deviating from what is straight or right; not straightforward; insincere, indirect, crooked.

The first is almost always used of behaviour. The second is less limited, and may be used of physical things (*We followed a devious route*, i.e. roundabout) or abstract ones (*a devious plot*, i.e. one with twists and turns).

see **diverge**.

deviate: see **deviant** and **diverge**.

device, devise The difference is the same as that between **advice, advise,** i.e. the first is the noun, the second the verb.

devoted, devout The similarity is that both mean *loyally attached, dedicated.* The difference is that the second has religious overtones and can mean *strongly religious*, as well as *sincere, heartfelt* in a more general way. A further and more subtle difference is that *devoted* implies loyalty in action whereas *devout* implies it more in attitude.

Devout includes the meaning of *devoted*, but *devoted* cannot express all that *devout* does (in, for example, *it is her devout hope that* . . .). But there is little difference between a *devout* and a *devoted* Christian or supporter of a cause.

The primary distinction is that between *a devoted daughter*, one who cares for her parents, and a *devout daughter*, one who has a strong religious commitment.

diagnosis, prognosis A *diagnosis* is an identification of the nature of an illness; a *prognosis* is a forecast of how it will develop. Both words are often applied (sometimes without due regard for their distinction) to other sorts of problems, such as economic or political ones.

dialogue, duologue, monologue Two people in conversation may be said to be having a *dialogue* or a *duologue*. If more than two are taking part, it can only be a *dialogue*. One person talking without interruption is holding a *monologue*.

dichotomy, difference *Dichotomy* is too much used by people who do not know what it means. It is a division, usually a clearly defined one, into two groups which are strongly contrasted or even opposed, and is generally used of abstractions such as ideas or systems of beliefs. It should not be used as if it meant merely *difference*, and certainly not as another word for *problem* or *ambiguity*.

For **difference** see also **differential**.

differential, difference Apart from its technical meaning in mathematics and science, a *differential* is a factor that makes a *difference*. A differential is not a difference: it is a perception or showing of difference. For example, there is a *difference* between the pay of nurses and doctors. Their pay *differential*, however, is more than that: it is the factor (i.e. the determination that different sorts of work should be differently rewarded) that brings about the difference in pay.

For **difference** see also **dichotomy**.

diffident: see **indifferent**.

dilemma, problem   Careful writers note that a *dilemma* is a position in which one is faced with *two* equally undesirable alternatives (the prefix *di-* implying two as in *dialogue*). Its use to signify a mere *problem* is standard but loose.

direct, directly   As well as being an adjective (*direct hit, direct consequence*, etc.) *direct* is an adverb, as *directly* is.

> *direct*:   straight, by the shortest way, without interruption.
> *directly*:   in a direct manner (*He answered me directly*, without equivocation); immediately.

There is thus an important difference between *Ask him to contact me direct* (i.e. not through an intermediary) and *Ask him to contact me directly* (at once).

disability: see **inability**.

disabled, incapacitated   Both mean *lacking power, strength or capacity*, but *disabled* usually means *permanently handicapped* whereas one can be *incapacitated* temporarily. Additionally *disabled* has to do with physical or mental impairment, whereas *incapacitated* is normally restricted to the physical.

disaffected: see **unaffected**.

disbar: see **debar**.

disbelief, unbelief   The first is the usual word for refusal or reluctance to believe something. *Unbelief* is a more formal word, usually restricted to doubt or lack of belief in a religion or cause.

See **disbeliever**.

disbeliever, unbeliever   Both lack belief (in a religion or cause) but a *disbeliever* positively rejects it whereas an *unbeliever* more neutrally abstains from it.

See **disbelief**.

disburse, disperse   Although these may be confused through careless pronunciation, they have no common meaning.

> *disburse*: make payment.
> *disperse*: scatter.

For the latter, see also **dispel**.

disc, disk   *Disc* is the English spelling, *disk* the American. The latter is now found much more frequently in print because of the spread of computer language (e.g. *floppy disk*). In all other contexts, however, *disc* is still to be preferred.

discomfort, discomfit, discomfiture Despite their similarity in spelling and pronunciation, the first two have little in common. *Discomfort* is the general word for lack of comfort: it also functions, more rarely, as a verb, often in the passive (*he was discomforted*, made uncomfortable). *Discomfit*, however, means *thwart, disconcert, embarrass* and the corresponding noun is *discomfiture*, the state of being frustrated, foiled or confused.

It is possible, indeed likely, that *discomfort* will accompany or be caused by one's *discomfiture*, but there is no necessary connexion.

discreditable: see **credible**.

discreet, discrete Indistinguishable by pronunciation, but with distinct meanings.

> *discreet*: unobtrusive, judiciously reserved in behaviour (*maintain a discreet silence*).
> *discrete*: separate; consisting of distinct parts (*ingredients remain discrete after cooking*).

The second is a rather technical term, originating in logic, and best reserved for learned contexts.

discrepancy, disparity Both mean *difference*, the first implying one that is wrong, the second one that merely exists.

> *discrepancy*: lack of consistency; disagreement; variation.
> *disparity*: lack of equality.

A tax officer spotting a *discrepancy* in one's tax returns is noting a difference between what should be and what is. To note a *disparity* between the earnings of a pop star and those of a surgeon is merely to state the fact of inequality, irrespective of what should be.

discrete: see **discreet**.

discriminating, discriminatory Both these adjectives come from the verb *discriminate* meaning *make or note a difference, distinguish*, but they have an important difference in sense. A *discriminating* person is one who is discerning, showing judgement and taste in differentiating. *Discriminatory* has unpleasant overtones: a *discriminatory* attitude shows unfairness, bias or prejudice.

As a verb, *discriminating* must be used with care, because *You are discriminating* means both *You are a person of discernment* and *You are prejudiced*.

disease: see **decease**.

disinterested, uninterested   Failure to understand the difference in this pair is a common source of error.

   Disinterested is not the opposite of *interested* as generally understood. It means *free from self-interest, impartial, free from bias. Uninterested* means *having or showing no interest.*

   A *disinterested* spectator at a football match supports neither side. An *uninterested* one is bored.

disk: see **disc**.

disorganised: see **unorganised**.

disoriented, disorientated   See **oriented, orientated**, of which these are the negative forms meaning *confused, having lost one's bearings.*

disparity: see **discrepancy**.

dispatch, despatch   Alternative spellings, the former being better as well as more common.

dispel, expel, disperse   All three have different senses of *get rid of. Dispel* and *expel* mean *drive out,* but *dispel* is used of abstractions (*dispel doubts/fears/suspicions*, etc.) and *expel* of people or physical things. *Disperse*, meaning *break up* or *scatter*, is often used of things so constituted that they can go or be sent in different directions (*the meeting/crowd/fog dispersed*) but there are contexts where it is interchangeable with *dispel.*

   For **disperse** see also **dispersal**.

dispersal, dispersion   *Dispersal* is the act of dispersing, *dispersion* the state of being dispersed. In practice *dispersal* is usually used for both, *dispersion* being limited to a few technical contexts, such as scientific ones, and to the Diaspora, the settlement of the Jews outside Palestine or Israel.

disperse: see **disburse**.

dispersion: see **dispersal**.

disposal, disposition   Among the meanings of *dispose* is *put in place, arrange,* as in *troops disposed around the building. Disposal* is the act of arranging or distributing, *disposition* the state of being arranged, though the latter usually does duty for both. Other meanings of *disposal* (*disposal of waste*, getting rid of it; *at one's disposal*, for one's use) and *disposition* (temperament, inclination) are not interchangeable.

dissatisfied, unsatisfied

dissatisfied: displeased, disappointed.

unsatisfied: not satisfied (*unsatisfied curiosity*).

If a meal leaves you *dissatisfied* you are discontented with what you have had; if you are *unsatisfied* you have not had enough. It is possible to be *unsatisfied* without being *dissatisfied*.

See **satisfactory**.

dissent, dissension, dissidence

dissent: difference of opinion, disagreement.

dissension: disagreement such as to cause discord or strife within a group.

dissidence: strong disagreement with established government or other general opinion.

dissimulate, simulate   Both have to do with *pretend* but

dissimulate: conceal by pretence (*dissimulate one's anger with a show of good temper*).

simulate: make pretence (*simulate anger*, pretend to be angry).

distinct, distinctive, distinguished   The essential difference is that of

distinguish (differentiate), *distinct* (distinguishable) and *distinctive* (distinguishing).

distinct: separate, clear, different (*a distinct nip in the air* is distinguishable).

distinctive: characteristic, serving to distinguish or mark out (*Chinese food has a distinctive taste*, distinguishing it from other food).

distinguished: differentiated, having a distinctive feature (*distinguished by its colour*, differentiated from others). Hence *The mountain has a distinct outline* (which makes it distinguishable from its surroundings) but *The mountain has a distinctive outline* (which distinguishes it, marking it out as different from others). The latter idea could be conveyed by *The mountain is distinguished by its outline*.

Distinguished, of course, also means *dignified in appearance* and *eminent*.

distract: see **detract**.

distraught, distrait Usually associated with anxiety but in very different degrees. *Distraught* means *frantic* whereas *distrait* (pronounced *dis-tray*) is *abstracted, absent-minded.*

distrust, mistrust Both words are negatives of *trust*, but *distrust* indicates a much stronger lack of trust than *mistrust* does. To mistrust someone's intentions is to feel doubt; to distrust them is to feel positive suspicion.

Mistrust is the form normally used if one is feeling doubt about oneself: *I mistrust myself* is more idiomatic than *I distrust myself.*

disturb, perturb Whereas it is possible to *disturb* persons or things, *perturb* can be used only of people, in the sense *cause confusion or disorder in mind or emotions of. Disturb* can mean this too, but is more usually reserved for physical disturbance (*Do Not Disturb*) to which *perturb* cannot be applied.

disused, unused
> *disused*: no longer in use (*disused factory*).
> *unused*: not used (*unused glass*, i.e. clean), new (*unused pair of shoes*), not used up (*unused pocket-money*).

diverge, deviate, divert Confusingly, all three can mean *turn aside from* (*a path or course*).

Diverge has the special sense of *move in different directions from the same starting point*. There is a sense of complete break: a path that diverges becomes two separate ones; opinions that diverge are irreconcilable.

Deviate never takes an object: one can deviate but not deviate something or be deviated. It means, literally, *turn away from a previous course* or, metaphorically, *change from a norm or a previously held belief.* After a deviation one may return to a normal course.

Divert (deflect) normally has an object: *decision to divert traffic from the shopping centre; diverted my attention from the matter in hand.*

divers, diverse Originally synonymous but no longer so. *Divers* is a little-used word for *several, various. Diverse* means *having marked differences.*

divert: see **diverge**.

divisive, dividing, divided
> *divisive*: causing division, disunity, disagreement, dissention, etc. (*a divisive policy/plan/action*).

dividing: (or things) making a division (*a dividing wall* between two rooms).

divided: having a division or divisions (*divided loyalties*, split between different causes).

dominate, predominate

dominate: exert control, influence; be in superior position.

predominate: be more important or numerous (*Spanish predominates in South America*).

The corresponding adjectives are *dominant* and *predominant*.

Predominate used to mean the same as *dominate*, but is hardly ever used in that way now.

See **dominating** and **predominate**.

dominating, domineering The notion of exercising control, authority or influence is common to both, but there is a significant difference. *Domineering* control is always overbearing, excessive, arbitrary and bullying. *Dominating* lacks that sense.

See **dominate**.

doubtful, dubious Generally interchangeable, though the construction *it is doubtful if* . . . is more idiomatic than *it is dubious if* . . . . *Dubious* is the stronger word, implying a greater measure of doubt. It is also the word that one is more likely to reach for to express uncertainty as to moral propriety (*a dubious business deal*). That is not to say that *dubious* always implies uncertainty verging on moral distrust: *I am dubious of* . . . is merely less tentative than *I am doubtful of* . . . .

douse, dowse Dictionaries give these as alternative spellings of the verb meaning *extinguish* (e.g. a light), *pour water over* or *plunge into liquid*. In practice, *douse* is the almost universal spelling, and *dowse* is reserved for *attempt to locate underground water with a divining-rod*, in which case it is pronounced to rhyme with *rouse*. *Douse* rhymes with *mouse*.

dower, dowry Only likely to be encountered in books referring to the past. A *dower* is a widow's legal share, during her lifetime, of her dead husband's property, whereas a *dowry* is the goods brought to a husband by a wife at marriage. Originally they were the same word.

dowse: see **douse**.

draught, draft Both have several meanings, of which the most

drawers, draws

common are:

  draught: current of air (*draught-excluder*); a drawing off from a cask (*draught beer*); the act of pulling a load (*draught-horse*); the depth of water needed for a ship to float.

  draft: sketch, outline (*rough draft of a letter*); order for payment of money (*banker's draft*); group of people (usually military) selected for a purpose.

American English uses *draft* for all of these, but this simplification shows no sign of catching on.

drawers, draws Careless pronunciation makes these sound alike, but they are quite different words. *Drawers* are sliding containers in tables, etc. (or old-fashioned undergarments). *Draws* are lotteries, attractions, or games ending in a tie.

dreamed, dreamt Both are acceptable as the past tense of dream, but *dreamt* is probably the more common, rhyming with *unkempt*.

drunk, drunken Both mean the same, but as adjectives *drunk* is normally used after a verb (*He became very drunk*) and *drunken* before the noun (*drunken behaviour*) though *drunken* appears to be on the wane: it has certainly been superseded in such common expressions as *drunk driving*.

dual, duel *Duel* is needed for *fight*, *dual* in all other cases (*dual purpose*, *dual carriageway*, etc.). It means *having two parts*.

dubious: see **doubtful**.

due to, owing to Controversy surrounds these expressions. Like it or not, observance of the generally accepted rules is still regarded as a sign of careful usage.

The problem centres on *due to*. It means *caused by*. Being adjectival, it must link with a specific and stated noun/pronoun (in the sentence) that is *caused by* something. Unless *due to* can be replaced by the words *caused by* and the sentence still make grammatical sense, its use is wrong.

His success was due to luck is correct. *All flights have been cancelled due to fog* is not: the only noun that *due to* can relate to is *flights*, and the *flights* have not been *caused by fog*. Never use *due to* unless there is a noun/pronoun it relates to. The answer to *what is due?* must be a word in the same sentence.

Due to causes so many problems, especially when it begins a sentence (*Due to fog, all flights are delayed*), that there is a good case for never

62

beginning a sentence with it unless you are confident of your grammar.

There are no such restrictions on *owing to* (*because of*) and its use in all contexts is normally safe: the same is true of *because of* and *on account of*. If in doubt, use *owing to*.

There is no problem when *due to* means *belonging to* (as in *the respect that is due to him*).

duel: see **dual**.

duologue: see **dialogue**.

duplicate: see **replica**.

E

earthly, earthy Found in a number of rather informal expressions such as *no earthly reason* (no reason on earth, i.e. at all) and *not an earthly* (*chance*) (no chance whatsoever), *earthly* means *characteristic of earth* (rather than heaven); *worldly, materialistic* as in *our earthly life*. *Earthy* means *characteristic of earth* in the sense of *soil*, etc. Vegetables may have a specially *earthy* taste or a person may have *an earthy sense of humour* (coarse, down-to-earth).

eatable, edible The distinction is between *good to eat/palatable* and *safe to eat*. Potatoes are *eatable*; if they are served raw or burnt, many people would find them *uneatable*. Those plants and fungi which may be eaten are *edible*; those which are poisonous, for example, are *inedible*.

Both words, and their negatives, are often used without regard for these distinctions, which are rather pointless.

eclectic, esoteric
> *eclectic*: having elements drawn from a variety of sources, styles, methods, opinions, etc. (*an eclectic taste in music/ food/books*).
>
> *esoteric*: understood by or intended for only a small group of initiates; difficult to understand for this reason (*an esoteric religious cult*).

economic, economical
> *economic*: having to do with economics, the science of the production and distribution of goods and services (*economic forces; the government's economic policy*).

> *economical*: having to do with economy in the sense of thrift (*need to be economical with our money*).

An *economic rate for the job* is a rate of pay determined by market forces, the availability of labour, the need to balance profit and loss, etc. An *economical rate* is a cheap one.

edify, educate   Both mean *instruct*, but *educate* is a very general word applying to all fields of knowledge, skill and experience, and to intellectual, aesthetic, physical, emotional and spiritual development. *Edify* is generally restricted to moral instruction: it is usually found in the adjectival form *edifying* (enlightening, improving) and the noun *edification*, a rather high-minded and threatening word for *instruction* or *benefit*.

educational, educative   If an experience contributes to our own education it matters little whether we call it *educational* or *educative*. Apart from that, the first is the more general word meaning *having to do with education* (*educational policy/development/aims*). The second is less common and more precise, meaning *tending to teach* (*an educative film/work/lecture*).

effect: see **affect**.

effective, effectual, efficacious, efficient   The first three have the broad meaning of *having a (desired) effect, producing an (intended) result*, but their usage differs.

Effective is the most common (and some say the only one needed). It means *practical, having a useful effect*: its uses can be seen in *an effective plan* (productive of the required result), *an effective speaker* (impressive) and *the effective head of the government* (not in theory but in practice).

Effectual stresses the ability to achieve results and is often used negatively (*not very effectual, ineffectual*), usually of people who are incapable of making much of an impression either in their work or in other ways. *Efficacious* stresses the potential to produce an effect, and is often applied to medicine, remedies, or treatment more generally.

Efficient stands apart from these three in meaning *producing a result in a desirable way* with the implication of speed, expertise, economy, smoothness, etc.

The corresponding nouns are *effectiveness, effectualness* (not much used), **efficacy** and *efficiency*.

effete, effeminate   The primary meaning of *effete* is *weak, exhausted, lacking vitality* (often applied to civilisations, schools of thought, etc.).

From this it has come to mean *decadent, worn out by too much refinement* and loosely *affected, listless, inclined to pose*. It has nothing to do with *effeminate (unmanly)* but is often used as if it has, especially in the language of polemic and abuse where the two words are often paired.

efficacious: see **effective**.

efficacy, effectiveness, efficiency Little difference exists between the first two (*capacity to produce a result*) except that *efficacy* tends to be used especially of remedial measures. *Efficiency* is the capacity to produce a *good* result with expertise, economy of effort, etc.

For a fuller description of the adjectives corresponding to these, see **effective**.

See **proficiency**.

efficient: see **effective**.

effluent: see **affluent**.

effrontery: see **affront**.

egoism, egotism Selfishness and preoccupation with the self characterise both, the distinction (widely ignored in practice) being that between *self-interest* and *self-importance*.

    egoism: dedication to self-seeking; excessive concern with one's own interests.

    egotism: self-centredness, conceit, boastfulness; talking about oneself too much.

The latter (together with the adjective *egotistical* and the noun *egotist*, an egotistical person) is the more common of the two.

Egoism (with *egoistical* and *egoist*) implies ruthlessness; *egotism* tends to invite mere irritation or derision.

The first syllable of all these words is pronounced *egg*.

elapse: see **lapse**.

elder, older These mean the same, and are used of two people only. For more than two, *eldest/oldest* are required. Only *elder* may be used as a noun meaning *a senior* (*elders and betters*) or occasionally *a senior official* (*an elder of the church*).

As adjectives, *elder* and *eldest* are used only of seniority within a family, usually one's own. They can only be used immediately before their noun (*my elder brother*). In other constructions *older/-est* are needed: *My brother is older than me; my sister is the one who is oldest.* The exception to this rule is the occasional use of *elder/-est* with the following noun omitted and 'understood' (*He is my eldest* i.e. eldest child; *He is the elder* e.g. *elder brother*).

Older/-est are not restricted to people in this way. They show signs of ousting *elder/-est* in their adjectival uses.

eldest: see **elder**.

elegy, eulogy   There is a slight possibility of confusion because an *elegy* is a mournful poem (or piece of music), often a funeral song, and a *eulogy* may be a funeral oration. Both words have more general meanings, however:

elegy: thoughtful or reflective poem. Any elegaic writing or music is mournful in tone.

eulogy: an expression of praise in speech or writing.

elemental, elementary   Although related in meaning *fundamental*, these are used quite distinctly. *Elementary* is the more familiar: it means *rudimentary, simple*. *Elemental* is much rarer: it has to do with the four elements – earth, air, fire and water – which are fundamental in nature. The meaning is *created by or comparable to powerful forces in nature* (as in *elemental passions/violence/beauty*).

elevator, escalator   Like many Americanisms, *elevator* in the sense of *lift* is gaining ground in Britain. Its main use, however, is still for anything that lifts some*thing*, e.g. an endless belt or a continuous chain of containers. It is also applied to part of the tailplane mechanism of an aircraft, aiding ascent and descent. An *escalator* is a moving staircase.

elicit, illicit   Pronounced in the same way, but otherwise unalike.

elicit: (verb):   draw out (response, answer, reaction, etc.).

illicit (adjective): unlawful; forbidden.

See **illegal**.

eligible, illegible   Perhaps confusable in sound, but not otherwise.

eligible: qualified or worthy to be chosen (*an eligible candidate/ bachelor*).

illegible: impossible to read

For **illegible** and **ineligible** see **illegible**.

elude, allude

elude: avoid, usually by cunning or skill (*elude one's pursuers*); escape (one's mind, memory, etc.), baffle (*His name eludes me*, I cannot remember his name).

allude: refer (to something) indirectly, casually, by implication.
See **allude, allusive, elusive** and **evade**.

elusive, illusory   The first is related to **elude**, the second to **illusion**.
elusive: difficult to understand, recall or express; difficult to get hold of.
illusory: unreal, deceptive.
There is a word *elusory* which means the same as *elusive*, but it is not much used.
See also **allusive**, **elude** and **evasive**.

emend: see **amend**.

emigrant, immigrant, emigré   All three denote a person who moves from one country to another. An *emigrant* is one who leaves a country, an *immigrant* one who enters. Both do both, of course: which word is used depends on the point of view; a person who leaves Britain for Australia is an emigrant in Britain and an immigrant in Australia.
An *emigré* is a person who has left his own country for (usually) political reasons. The word denotes distinction of status, frequently that of an intellectual.
See **migrate**.

emigrate: see **migrate**.

eminent, imminent, immanent
eminent: distinguished.
imminent: impending.
immanent: inherent, indwelling.
The last two are close in pronunciation, but confusion is unlikely as *immanent* is seldom heard. It is a rather theological adjective, often used to describe the inescapable and pervading power or presence of God in creation.

emotive, emotional   Some dictionaries define these as synonyms in certain contexts, but in practice they are clearly differentiated. Both are to do with emotion as distinct from reason.
emotive: arousing emotion (usually strong, often of anger). An *emotive issue* causes passions to rise.
emotional: experiencing or showing emotion, sometimes excessive. An *emotional person/scene/dispute* is one that displays emotion.

empathy: see **sympathy**.

emulate, imitate

emulate, imitate Both mean *try to be like*. *Emulate* has the additional sense of *try to surpass* and may imply striving, rivalry or competition. *Imitate* merely implies copying.

enclave: see **conclave**

endemic, epidemic, pandemic All these are both adjectives and nouns, but the first is usually found as an adjective and the other two as nouns. *Endemic* means *present in a certain area or in certain people*: it may be applied to a disease or used more generally, usually of something disagreeable (*sense of failure endemic in young unemployed people*). An *epidemic* is something, usually but not necessarily a disease, that affects many people simultaneously. A *pandemic* is a disease affecting a wide area (such as a whole continent) and a very large number of people.

endorse, indorse, approve All mean *agree to or with*, but *endorse* is slightly more formal than *approve*, and can additionally mean *sign by way of agreement*. It can also mean *record conviction on* a driving licence. *Indorse* is a little-used variant spelling of *endorse*.

enervate, energise Because *energise* means *put energy into, invigorate* it is sometimes thought that *enervate* must mean *put (strong) nerve into*. It does not: it means the opposite – *deprive of vitality*.

English: see **British**.

enormity, enormousness An *enormity* is great wickedness or a monstrous crime. It has come, quite recently, to be used as a substitute for *something very big* in a way that is at best informal and at worse misleading. Does *the enormity of the losses* mean that they were enormous, or quite small but criminally brought about? There are plenty of words that convey the idea of hugeness or *enormousness*, and *enormity* is best restricted to its original meaning.

enquire, inquire Variant spellings. *Inquire* seems the more logical (and is the American) spelling but *enquire* is probably more common.
   However, a useful distinction between the two words is becoming established and is worth observing (though it is not wrong to regard the words as interchangeable):
        enquire (about): ask.
        inquire (into):   investigate.
   See **enquiry** and **query**.

enquiry, inquiry It is still correct to regard these as alternative

68

spellings, but there is a useful distinction that is now well established (and better established than that between **enquire, inquire**):

enquiry: request for information.

inquiry: investigation (*a public inquiry into the cause of the accident*).

For **inquiry** see **query**.

ensure: see **assure**.

enthralling: see **thrilling**.

entomology: see **etymology**.

envelop, envelope   *Envelop* (conceal, surround, enclose) is the verb, pronounced with the accent on the second syllable. *Envelope* is the noun for a wrapper or cover, especially a container for a letter, and is pronounced with the accent on the first syllable. Pronunciation of the first syllable as *on-*, or nasalised in the French manner, is old-fashioned and unnecessary: the word was originally French but is now thoroughly naturalised.

enviable, envious

enviable: worthy of envy (*an enviable reputation*).

envious: showing envy (*an envious glance*).

environs, environment   These used to mean the same (*surrounding area*) but *environment* now popularly refers to the conditions, usually the physical ones, in which people live, and *environs* to the outskirts of a town or city.

eon: see **era**.

epidemic: see **endemic**.

epigram, epigraph, epitaph

epigram: a short, witty saying, remark or poem.

epigraph: an inscription on a statue or building; a quotation at the front of a book or beginning of a chapter.

epitaph: an inscription on a gravestone; something that commemorates or is a final judgement on a person or thing.

The prefix *epi–* means *upon*, *above*, *over*.

epoch: see **era**.

equable, equitable

equable, equitable

> *equable*: uniform, even (*an equable climate*), not easily disturbed (*an equable temperament*).
>
> *equitable*: just, fair (*an equitable settlement*).

Equable always implies moderation, and could not be applied to, for example, a climate or temperament that is unvaryingly harsh.

era, epoch, aeon (eon)   The first two denote a long period of time with a distinctive character, or (less frequently) a point of time reckoned as the beginning of such a period, or (loosely) any long period of time (*the modern era*). *Era* is the more common word, especially found in *end of an era*, often marked by a death or defeat. *Epoch* is especially found in *epoch-making*, applied to an event marking the beginning of a new age; loosely it is used to mean *very significant.*

An *aeon* (of which *eon* is the less common version) is an immeasurably or indefinitely long period of time.

erosion: see **corrosion**.

erotic, exotic

> *erotic*: associated with, marked by or arousing sexual desire or excitement.
>
> *exotic*: foreign; attractively unusual or bizarre.

erupt, irrupt

> *erupt*: burst out or release suddenly, usually violently (*volcano/ street-fighting/anger erupted*).
>
> *irrupt*: enter forcibly or violently (*angry crowd irrupted through the doors*).

escalator: see **elevator**.

esoteric: see **eclectic**.

especial: see **special**.

especially, specially

> *especially*: notably, exceptionally, above all, in particular, to a high degree.
>
> *specially*: specifically, for a particular purpose.

Specially is usually found with verbs (*called specially to see me*). *Especially* is more flexible, being applicable to adjectives (*especially good*), adverbs (*drove especially dangerously*) and verbs (*I especially like cucumber*). There are occasions when either word may be used: there is no noticeable difference between *bought especially for you* (for you above all) and *specially for you* (for you specifically), but the words are usually distinguishable, certainly in writing, however often they may sound alike in speech.

essay: see **assay**.

et al., etc Two useful abbreviations of Latin expressions. *Et al.* is best reserved to mean *and other people*, and *etc.* to mean *and other things* (not people) because, strictly speaking, the original *et cetera* means *and the rest of the things*.

As the *et* in both expressions means *and*, it is never correct to say *and et al.* or *and etc.*

ethic, ethics, morals Philosophy apart, and in everyday language, these apply to differences between good and evil, right and wrong. *Morals* are generally recognised principles of good and bad as they apply to and are demonstrated in personal conduct. They are especially used of sexual conduct. *Ethics* are the rules of correct behaviour as recognised by a particular group or profession, such as scientists or doctors.

An *ethic* is a moral rule observed by some but not others. The *work ethic*, for instance, is the belief, demonstrated by one's actions, that hard work is intrinsically more valuable than other activity, such as leisure. An *ethic* does not have the same general validity as *morals* do.

See **amoral** and **moral**.

ethical: see **ethic**, **moral** and **amoral**.

etymology, entomology
    etymology: the study of the sources, history and meaning of words.
    entomology: the study of insects.

eulogy: see **elegy**.

euphemism, euphuism *Euphemism* is the use of a mild, imprecise or reassuring word or expression in place of one that would be offensive or unpleasantly specific. It is a device much resorted to by politicians seeking to disguise unpopular measures or their own mistakes, though it is often found in everyday use, such as when a sick pet is *put down* rather than *killed*.

Euphuism is not much used outside works of literary history or criticism: it is a style of writing that is very artificial and ornate.

71

evade, elude   The first has unpleasant associations. Like *elude* it means *get or keep away from* but the sense is *from disagreeable consequences for oneself* or *in an underhand way*. *Elude* may simply mean *escape from*; the context may imply *with skill or cunning* but not usually *with dishonesty*. For example, *His name eludes me* just means *His name has slipped my memory*. *He evaded me* means that he avoided me out of guilt or cowardice.

   See **evasion** and **avoidance**.

evasion, evasiveness   *Evasion* is something one does; *evasiveness* is something one has. The first is the act of evading (see **evade**), a piece of deception. The second is the quality of not being straightforward. If you ask someone a question, his *evasion* would be his failure to give a (straight) answer, his *evasiveness* the temperament or mentality he showed in dodging it. In other words, one speaks of his *evasion of* the question and his *evasiveness in* answering it.

   See **avoidance** and **evade**.

evasive, elusive   See **evade, elude** for the difference between the verbs corresponding to these adjectives.

event, eventuality   An *event* may be a happening (*a well-organised event*) or a possible happening (*in the event of fire.* . . . ; *in any event*, i.e. whatever may happen). As an *eventuality* too is a possible happening it is an unnecessary word. *Event* is always to be preferred.

everyday, every day   *Everyday* is adjectival, meaning *happening all the time, commonplace, usual, ordinary* (*an everyday occurrence*). *Every day* is an adverbial phrase meaning *all the time, on each day* as in *There is a delivery every day*.

everyone, every one   *Everyone* is a pronoun meaning *everybody, every person*. *Every one* means *every single one* (*person or thing*): the emphasis is on the separateness of what is being referred to whereas *everyone* stresses the totality (*We went to six shops and every one was closed*).

evince, evoke
   evince: show clearly, reveal (*He evinced no surprise*).
   evoke: summon up (*The house evoked happy memories*).
   Both are applied to qualities, such as emotions, or abstractions rather than objects. *Evoke* is specially used of feelings awakened from the past.
   For **evoke** see also **provoke**.

exacerbate, exasperate   Although some dictionaries define these as virtual synonyms, they are quite distinct in everyday use. *Exacerbate* is applied to things (e.g. hostility, a problem, a quarrel) and means *make worse*.

    Exasperate is applied to people and means *irritate, provoke*.

exalt, exult, extol   *Exult* (express joy or triumph) cannot have a direct object. *Exalt* usually does: it has two meanings – *raise high* (a person in rank) and *glorify, praise highly* – though *extol* is the more common word for this latter meaning.

    The nouns *exaltation*, which can mean *sense of uplift*, and *exultation*, which means *sense of joy*, are obviously close and need to be distinguished.

example, sample   *Example* has a number of meanings, but the one that approximates to that of *sample* is *something typical or illustrative of a larger group or type*. The difference, which is slight, is that an *example* illustrates quality (*an example of how he normally behaves*) whereas a *sample* is a small part, often extracted, that is representative of the whole (*a sample of blood, statistics based on a sample of the population*). An *example* is usually a single thing; a *sample* tends to have volume.

exasperate: see **exacerbate**.

exceed, excel   Both can mean *surpass* or *be superior to*. *Excel* is normally used in the sense of *be better than*: to *excel oneself* is to do better than one has previously done, and to *excel at* something is to perform to a higher standard than most people. *Exceed* means *be greater than* or *go beyond the limits of*, as when something *exceeds one's expectations* or someone *exceeds the speed limit*.

    For **exceed** see also **accede**.

exceedingly, excessively   Loosely used to mean *very*, these are in fact distinguishable.

      exceedingly: very greatly.

      excessively: too greatly.

    Excessively carries the sense of going beyond what is normal, adequate or allowed.

excel: see **exceed**.

except, excepting   *Except* is used to exclude a particular person or thing (or some persons or things) from a larger group or category (*Everyone was there except him*). *Except for* is normal at the beginning of a sentence (*Except for him, everyone was there*) and also when it is necessary to modify a whole statement in order to make a reservation (*Everyone would have been there except for the weather*). Generally it is rather informal to use *except for* if *except* will suffice.

Excepting is used only when preceded by *not, always*, or *without*, as in *Everyone is entitled to vote, always excepting* (i.e. with the exception of) *the chairman*.

For **except** see also **exempt** and **accept**.

exceptional, exceptionable The difference is that between *forming an exception* and *to which exception might be taken*. In plain terms:

> *exceptional*: unusual; superior.
> *exceptionable*: objectionable.

See also **unexceptional**.

excerpt: see **extract**.

excess: see **access**.

excessively: see **exceedingly**.

excite, incite Both mean *stimulate to action* but the emphasis in *excite* is on the arousal of response (pity, curiosity, passion, for example) whereas the emphasis in *incite* is on more vigorous provocation of people to do something (*incited the crowd to violence*).

excoriate: see **execrate**.

excuse: see **alibi**.

execrate, excoriate

> *execrate*: detest; express detestation of.
> *excoriate*: censure vehemently.

The second is rarer and stronger than the first, which is often found in the adjectival form *execrable*, abominable.

executor, executive An *executor* is a person nominated to execute (carry out) someone's last will and testament. An *executive* executes (administers) the work of a business or institution (as distinct from forming policy, law, etc.). *Executive* has also become a modish adjective suggestive of thrustful entrepreneurial trendiness (*executive briefcase, executive homes*, etc.).

exempt, except As verbs, both mean *exclude* but

> *exempt*: release from obligation (*low-income families exempted from paying tax*).

except: leave out, omit (*The other driver involved in the accident was excepted from blame*).

For **except** see **accept** and **except**.

exercise: see **exorcise**.

exhaustive, exhausting
> *exhaustive*: thorough, comprehensive.
> *exhausting*: causing exhaustion, tiring out; using up.

Both are applied to things (e.g. work, study, research) but the first describes the thing itself, the second its effect on people. A police search may be *exhaustive* in its meticulousness and *exhausting* for those taking part in it. Only *exhausting* may be applied to a person – if, for example, his behaviour wears you out.

exigent, exiguous Unfamiliar words, perhaps more likely to be confused for that reason.
> *exigent*:   exacting, demanding; urgent; pressing.
> *exiguous*: scanty, meagre.

In pronunciation, the stress is on the first and the second syllable respectively.

The sense of *exigent* is more often found in the noun *exigency*, usually in the plural *exigencies* (urgent necessity imposed by circumstances).

existent: see **extant**.

exorcise, exercise Because of imprecise pronunciation it is occasionally thought that the second, which is familiar enough, covers the meaning of the first. It does not, of course. *Exorcise* means *expel* (evil spirit) *from* (person or place) or *free* (person or place) *from* (evil spirit). *Exercise* has quite different meanings.

exotic: see **erotic**.

expect: see **anticipate**.

expedient, expeditious As adjectives:
> *expedient*:   advisable, suitable to the circumstances, having to do
> with what is advantageous or politic rather than just
> or fair; characterised by self-interest.
> *expeditious*: prompt, speedy.

Expedient also exists as a noun covering the same range of meanings.

expel: see **dispel**.

expiry, expiration

expiry, expiration For *termination*, especially of an agreement (e.g. a contract or lease), either word will do, *expiry* being the more common. *Expiration* has the additional sense *breathing out*.

explicit, implicit That which is *explicit* is openly and fully expressed. That which is *implicit* is not expressly stated but hinted at indirectly; it may be clearly understood or taken for granted without being asserted in so many words.

expound: see **propound**.

extant, existent Both mean *existing at the present time* but *extant* additionally implies survival.

extempore, impromptu If a speech, performance or action is done on the spur of the moment it may be described as either *extempore* or *impromptu*. Some argue that there is a distinction, *extempore* being applied to something known of in advance or partly anticipated but done without being fully prepared (e.g. a performance delivered without rehearsal, or a speech without notes or unmemorised), *impromptu* meaning *done at a moment's notice*, i.e. not only without preparation but also without advance warning. Such a distinction seems hardly worth preserving.

extensive, intensive It is a common error to use *intensive* (employing much effort) instead of *extensive* (widespread). The first is qualitative, the second quantitative.
See **intense**.

extenuate, attenuate
    extenuate: lessen seriousness (e.g. of offence) by excuses. *Extenuating circumstances* mitigate a fault.
    attenuate: lessen force, severity or vitality of; weaken, diminish; become thin, fine or weak by being extended.
The *-tenuate* part of both verbs has to do with thinness.

exterior, external As adjectives, both mean *on the outside* and in some contexts they are interchangeable (*paint suitable for exterior/external use*). Generally, however, *exterior* implies the existence of a corresponding opposite, *interior*. *External* has a wider range of application: it can mean *coming from outside* (*an external force*) or *involving foreign nations* (*external relations*); in medicine or anatomy it can mean *acting from the outside* (*medicine for external application*) or *on the outside of the body* (*an*

76

external wound); in philosophy it can mean *existing independently of the mind* (*external reality*). *Exterior* would be unidiomatic in such cases.

extol: see **exalt**.

extract, excerpt, abstract   Either *extract* or *excerpt* (as nouns) may be used to denote a quoted passage (from a book, film, piece of music, etc). *Extract* is more likely to be used of something which is to be read and *excerpt* of something to be seen or heard. *Excerpt* is also more likely to be used of an artistic performance and *extract* of something more factual.

An *abstract* is a summary of points (from a report, speech, argument, etc.).

For **extract** see also **extricate**.

extricate, extract   The common meaning is *remove* (person or thing) *usually with an effort*. *Extricate* has the sense of *disentangle* (e.g. from a difficulty) and *extract* the more straightforward sense of *pull out*.

For **extract** see also **extract**.

exult: see **exalt**.

F

fabled, fabulous   Both mean *occurring or celebrated in fable* and hence *legendary, incredible*, though *fabulous* has been so overworked as a popular term of general approval that it has come to mean little more than *very good*. *Fabled* is a variant that is both more modest and less hackneyed: it means *highly reputed* and also, rarely, *fictitious*.

facility, faculty   A *facility* is ease, apitude or dexterity; it is also a provision (e.g. buildings or equipment) useful for a purpose, and in this sense it is often found in the plural *facilities* meaning much the same as *amenities*. A *faculty* is an ability or capability, especially an inherent power of the mind or body such as speech or memory. The distinction, not always observed, is that a person who has a *faculty* for mathematics or chess has an innate ability, whereas someone who has a *facility* in them has acquired it by practice or experience. *Facility* is specially used of manual skill.

A *faculty* is also a body of teachers.

faction, fraction *Fraction*, meaning *part, subdivision, fragment*, may refer to people (*a small fraction of the population*) but more usually applies to things. A *faction* is a group of people within and usually dissenting from a larger group. *Faction* is also strife or dissension within a group.

See also **factious**.

factious, fractious *Factious* is the adjective from **faction** and thus means *forming an identifiable group within a larger one*; the word is associated with dissent. *Fractious* usually means *irritable* though it can also mean *unruly*.

factitious, fictitious, fictional Three words that have similarities in meaning as well as sound. *Factitious*, an uncommon word, means *artificially engineered or manufactured*, i.e. not spontaneously or naturally, hence *unreal*, as one might create *factitious* popularity for a product by widespread advertising. *Fictitious* also means *unreal* but in the sense of *feigned, untrue, not genuine, sham, invented*: a *fictitious* name or address is a false one. Something that is *factitious* really exists; something that is *fictitious* does not.

Fictional means *pertaining to or existing in published fiction*: a fictional character is one in a book, play, film, etc. *Fictional* relates to *fiction*, meaning literature, whereas *fictitious* relates to *a fiction*, meaning an untruth.

failing: see **foible**.

faint, feint Although pronounced alike, these words do not overlap in their meanings. A *feint* is a movement designed to mislead: a footballer may *make a feint* (or simply *feint*, because the word is also a verb) to go in one direction and then, having wrong-footed his opponents, set off in another. The word is also a printing term denoting the narrowest line on ruled paper.

A *faint* is a loss of consciousness. The word also exists as an adjective and a verb with familiar meanings.

fallacious, fallible *Fallacious* can be applied only to things: it means *tending to mislead, containing a fallacy* (i.e. a false idea or argument); hence a *fallacious argument* is unsoundly based and therefore deceptive. *Fallible*, meaning *capable of making a mistake*, may be applied to people (*a fallible witness*) or things (*a fallible memory*).

falseness, falsity, falsehood All three refer to the quality of being false or untrue. *Falsehood* is the normal word for a lie or the act of lying. The other two are generally interchangeable (e.g. in signifying invalidity in an argument) but *falseness* denotes a false state, *falsity* a false action. Additionally, *falsity* implies deception and *falseness* treacherousness.

fantastic, fantastical   *Fantastic* means *imaginary*, or *extravagantly eccentric and grotesque*, especially in appearance. Informally it means *incredible*, especially in size; very informally it means *extremely good* as a general, rather slangy term of enthusiastic approval. *Fantastical* means *having the characteristics of fantasy*: it corresponds to the formal meanings of *fantastic*, especially to the second one quoted.

See **fantasy**.

fantasy, phantasm   Both are illusions and products of the imagination. A *phantasm* is also a ghost. *The fantasy* is the imagination, unrestricted by reality. *A fantasy* is a creation of the imagination, especially when bizarre or elaborate and written down as a story with grotesque and unrealistic features. The word can also mean *day-dream*.

Fantasy may spelt *phantasy*, but it seldom is.

See **phantom**.

farther, further   As adverbs, both mean *to or at a greater distance in space or time*. As adjectives they mean *more distant*. Some argue that *farther* is best for literal distance (*I can't walk any farther*) and *further* for figurative uses (*Nothing was further from my mind*) but few people observe this unnecessary distinction and in practice the words are interchangeable. *Further* is much the more common form, perhaps because it has several uses denied to *farther*. Only *further* can mean *additional* (*without further ado*) and *additionally* or *moreover* (*he further stated. . .*) or be used as a verb meaning *help along* (*further one's career*).

fatal, fateful, fated   In the sense of *having or producing unpleasant consequences* the first two words are generally interchangeable: a momentous decision, for instance, may be either *fatal* or *fateful* if its outcome is disastrous. *Fatal* is normal if death is the outcome (*a fatal accident*); it is also a common word for *ruinous* (*a fatal mistake*) and, by overuse, has become weakened to mean little more than *unfortunate* in some contexts. *Fateful* has the sense of *governed by fate* which is shared by *fated* (*destined, doomed*), though *fateful* signifies *decisive, important for the future*.

fearful, fearsome
    fearful: feeling fear.
    fearsome: causing fear.

feasible, probable

It is possible for *fearful* to mean the same as *fearsome* (*He was in a fearful temper*) and to be commonly and loosely used to mean *very great* or *very unpleasant* (*They had a fearful row*).

feasible, probable   If something is *feasible* it can be done: it is possible. The word has also come to mean *probable* or likely. A serious misunderstanding may arise if a speaker intends *possible* and a hearer understands *probable*; therefore use *feasible* with care, or avoid it.

feckless, reckless   Both mean *irresponsible* but in different senses. *Reckless* implies the taking of risks, careless of the consequences, while *feckless* implies mere feebleness of character. *Feckless* also means *weak, ineffectual*.

feint: see **faint**.

felonious: see **nefarious**.

female, feminine   *Female* denotes the sex of a person, animal or plant. *Feminine* is the less specific term suggesting the more general qualities or characteristics of womanhood.

ferment, foment   Apart from its chemical meaning, a *ferment* (pronounced with the stress on the first syllable) is a state of upheaval, unrest and agitation. The verb *ferment* (pronounced with the stress on the second syllable) means *to be in a state of commotion* or *seethe* (*Resentment of the government has been fermenting for years*) or *to cause to be in a commotion*. In this latter case the verb cannot be applied to people, i.e. one may *ferment discord* but not *ferment a crowd*, though a crowd may be *in a ferment* (noun).

Foment (pronounced with the stress on the second syllable) is a verb only. It means *incite, stir up* and is usually applied to trouble (*to foment rebellion*). Like *ferment* it cannot be applied to people. Unlike *ferment*, however, it must be used transitively, i.e. one must foment something; one cannot say *unrest has been fomenting* (though there is nothing wrong with *unrest has been fomented*, which is a straightforward passive).

There is thus no difference between fermenting a riot and fomenting it, though *foment* is probably slightly more common in this transitive use.

fervent, fervid, perfervid   The first two mean *intensely passionate*, but *fervid* has acquired some of the tone of *perfervid* (*excessively impassioned or zealous*) and thus has faint connotations of disapproval that *fervent* lacks. To call a supporter of a cause *fervent* is to define him as ardent: to call him *fervid* is to imply that his zeal is slightly unhealthy. Another difference is that *fervid* tends to be restricted to people whereas *fervent* may be applied to things, such as hopes and wishes. But both these differences are small and by no means widely acknowledged.

festival, festivity, festive, festal Of the two nouns, *festivity* is the general term for merry-making, *festival* denoting a more specific occasion for celebration, often of a cultural or religious nature.

Of the adjectives, *festive* corresponds to *festivity* and means *joyous, celebratory*, though *festival* may be used in this sense without the limitation to cultural or religious events that characterises the use of *festival* as a noun (*a festive/festival atmosphere*). *Festal* is a much rarer and more formal variant, restricted to defining solemn or religious rite.

fewer, fewest: see **less, fewer**.

fiction: see **figment**.

fictional: see **factitious**.

fictitious: see **factitious**.

figment, fiction A *figment*, like *fiction*, is something imagined or fabricated, but whereas *fiction* is literature or (usually in the form of *a fiction*) an untruth, a *figment* (which is seldom found outside the expression *a figment of one's imagination*) is a piece of fantasy or self-delusion and is not necessarily intended to mislead others.

first, firstly Whatever some grammar books may say, it does not matter whether you begin a series of points with *First, Second, Third*. . . or *Firstly, Secondly, Thirdly*. . . though it is tidier to keep to one sequence or the other, and not mix the two (*First, Secondly*. . .). The shorter version is, as usual, probably better.

flagrant: see **blatant**.

flail: see **flay**.

flair, flare The notion of brilliance, common to both, and identical pronounciation may aid confusion here. *Flair* is the word for intuitive aptitude, perceptiveness or stylishness. *Flare* is the noun and verb associated with flames and the (usually) figurative *flare(-)up*.

flammable: see **inflammable**.

flaunt, flout, vaunt The first two are frequently confused, not only

flavour

because of their similarities of sound but perhaps also because they both denote an assertive and usually disagreeable attitude of mind, though in fact it is *flaunt* and *vaunt* that are closest in meaning.

flaunt: display ostentatiously (*flaunt one's wealth*).

flout: display contempt for (*flout the rules of the game*).

vaunt: display or describe proudly or boastfully (*vaunting ambition*).

Flaunt is normally used disparagingly.

flavour: see **savour**.

flay, flail A *flail* is an implement for threshing grain; as a verb it means *beat (as if) with a flail* or *thresh about with wild movements of arms (or fists)*. It has no connection with *flay* (strip off the skin, e.g. by whipping; criticise savagely).

fleeting, flying These share the sense of *rapid and brief* but are not generally interchangeable. *Flying* is largely confined (in this sense) to *flying visit* but *fleeting* has wider applications: *fleeting glimpse/glance/pleasure/years/memories*, etc.

fleshly, fleshy

fleshly: relating to the flesh; carnal; worldly as opposed to spiritual (*fleshly desires*).

fleshy: consisting of flesh; plump, corpulent (*fleshy features*).

flinch: see **wince**.

flotsam, jetsam Both are cargo or wreckage of a lost ship, but *flotsam* floats and *jetsam* is either jettisoned (i.e. thrown overboard) or washed up on shore.

Figuratively, *flotsam and jetsam* together may be odds and ends, or vagrants.

flounder, founder Easily confused, both being associated with difficulty or failure.

flounder: move with a struggle, as in water or mud; make mistakes as if likely to be overwhelmed by events.

founder: sink; collapse; fail.

People flounder; things founder.

flowed, flown The first is a verb-form of *flow*, the second of *fly*.

flush: see **blush**.

flying: see **fleeting**.

foible, failing Both denote a minor shortcoming in character, but *foible* is the gentler word signifying a little quirk that may even be endearing.

follow: see **succeed**.

font, fount Either will do to denote the full range of types and sizes of letters in printing: *fount* is the more usual, *font* being preferred in American English. Otherwise:

font: receptacle for holy water in church.

fount: fountain; source.

forbear, forebear

forbear (verb):   refrain from; be patient. (Pronounced with stress on the second syllable.)

forebear (noun): ancestor. (Pronounced with stress on first syllable, sounding *for*.)

Dictionaries give *forbear* as a variant spelling of *forebear* but it is logical to insist on *forebear*, easily remembered by analogy with many *fore-* words in which *fore-* has the sense of *before, in front*, such as *foreground, forecast, forearm, forecourt, forefather*, etc.

forbidding, foreboding *Forbidding* is an adjective meaning *discouraging, unfriendly, ominous, threatening (a forbidding manner/building/ appearance)*. *Foreboding* may be an adjective, also meaning *threatening (evil)*, but it is almost always used as a noun meaning *a feeling of impending unpleasantness or evil, an omen*, as in *He was filled with foreboding*.

forceful, forcible Interchangeable in the sense of *convincing, effective*, though *forceful* is more frequently found. Additionally, *forcible* means *done by force (forcible entry, a forcible reminder)* and *forceful* has the sense *full of force, powerful, vigorous* as in *a forceful argument/personality/speaker*.

forego, forgo *Forego* (go before) is found in the forms *foregone (a foregone conclusion*, a conclusion that is determined in advance, therefore inevitable) and *foregoing* which can be an adjective (*the foregoing pages*, the previous ones) or a noun (*the foregoing*, the previous part).

Forgo means *do without, give up*. Dictionaries record that it may be spelt *forego*, but it is logical to retain this spelling for *go before* by analogy with other words which begin with *fore-*: this prefix commonly means *before* or *in front* (see **forbear**). It is therefore recommended that the spellings *forego* and *forgo* are kept separate.

83

forever, for ever The admission of *forever* into British English has been resisted, but no-one now seriously questions it. Careful writers, however, distinguish between *for ever* (for all time) and *forever* (at all times, persistently). Thus *He said he would love her for ever* but *He's forever complaining*.

formerly, formally
> *formerly*: in the past; in a *former* time.
> *formally*: officially; in a *formal* manner.

formulae, formulas Either of these plurals of *formula* is acceptable, though *formulae* is normal in maths and science and *formulas* in more general speech and writing. Foreign plurals (such as *formulae*) quite commonly come to be ousted by English ones taking the normal -*s* ending.

> *Formulae* is usually pronounced so that the final syllable rhymes with *bee*.

fortuitous, fortunate An occurrence may be both *fortuitous* (accidental) and *fortunate* (lucky), but it does not follow that the words mean the same, despite the complication that *fortuitous* has overtones of *happening by lucky chance*. The basic emphasis is on pure chance in *fortuitous*, good fortune in *fortunate*.

forward, forwards *Forward* is the usual word (except in the phrase *backwards and forwards*) and is an adverb (*move forward*), adjective (*forward movement*), noun (a *forward* in football) and verb (*forward a letter*).

> *Forwards* is a variant spelling in the adverbial sense only (*move forwards*) but is best avoided, as no clear rules can be formulated for its use: one would never say, for example, *No-one came forwards to volunteer* though *The car was moving forwards* is acceptable.

founder: see **flounder**.

fount: see **font**.

fraction: see **faction**.

fractious: see **factious**.

frantic, frenetic Meaning *showing frenzy, agitation, mental derangement*, there is little to choose between these two, though *frantic* has an emphasis on desperation, *frenetic* on hectic movement.

fruition, fruit Figuratively, *fruit* is the result, usually favourable, of an action or effort (often found in the plural, *the fruits of one's labour*) and *fruition* is the fulfilment of something worked for. Common expressions include *bear fruit* and *come to fruition,* both meaning *succeed.*

fulsome, copious *Fulsome* is often thought to be, and used as if it were, an alternative to *copious* in describing, for example, praise or thanks. It is not.
> *fulsome*: disgustingly excessive, insincere, servile, etc.; gross; cloying.
> *copious*: plentiful.

In other words, *fulsome* has disparaging connotations, and *copious* has not.

funereal, funerary *Funereal* (like or of a funeral) is almost always found in a figurative context (*speak in a funereal voice, traffic moved at a funereal pace*). *Funerary* (used for or associated with a funeral) is almost always literal (*a funerary urn*) and rather scholarly: the noun *funeral* is often used as an adjective instead (*a funeral urn*).

further: see **farther**.

fuse, fuze It is doubtful if the distinction is worth preserving, but
> *fuse*: part of electric circuit, usually a piece of wire, designed to melt and break the circuit in the event of overload.
> *fuze*: device used to detonate explosion in a bomb, firework, rocket, etc.

Most dictionaries regard *fuze* as American English, and *fuse* as having both meanings.

G

Gaelic: see **Celtic**.

gaffe, gaff Some dictionaries list these as alternative spellings of the noun meaning *blunder*, but most insist on *gaffe* and restrict *gaff* to various nautical and angling appliances. There is also a slang expression *blow the gaff* meaning *disclose a secret.*

Gallic: see **Celtic**.

gamble, gambol Despite their identical pronunciation and sense of frivolity, the words are quite distinct.

goal, jail

> *gamble*: risk.
> *gambol*: frolic
> Both are verbs and nouns.

gaol, jail   Both spellings are acceptable, *jail* being the more common and straightforward (and the only possible one in American English). The same is true of the derivatives *jailer, jailbreak, jailbird*, etc.

gargantuan, gigantic   *Gargantuan* is one of those words which have entered the language by being derived from the name of a fictional character: Gargantua was a giant with an appetite to match. *Gargantuan* is therefore best applied to quantities of food and drink, to size, or to words such as *helpings, portion, thirst*. It does not have the flexibility of *gigantic* and would sound odd if used to describe such words as *failure, cost, mountains*, etc. as *gigantic* readily can.

genetic, generic

> *genetic*: having to do with the origin and variation of organisms
>   in animals or plants.
> *generic*: characteristic of a class; general, not specific.

genius, genie, genii   The plural of *genius* is *geniuses* except on the rare occasions when it is used in its mythological senses to mean a guiding or guardian spirit or a demon, in which case the normal plural is *genii*. A *genie* is a sprite or goblin (sometimes called a *jinn*) in Arabic mythology: its plural too is *genii*, though *genies* exists and is better.

It is possible, though quite unnecessary, to use *genii* as the plural of *genius* in its familiar senses.

genteel, gentle   These have a common origin but have sharply diverged. *Gentle* is too familiar to need definition, but *genteel* is more complex, carrying as it does something of the original meaning of *gentle* (well-born) that survives in *gentle birth* and *gentleman of leisure*. *Genteel* is often used ironically or disparagingly to mean *characteristic of the upper classes* or *affectedly refined*, but it can be used quite straightforwardly to describe the behaviour of people who are maintaining or trying to maintain old-fashioned standards of respectability and politeness of the kind which is appropriate to a good social class, or is thought to be.

gerontocracy, gerontology

> *gerontocracy*: government by old men.
> *gerontology*: the study of aging and the aged.

gesture, gesticulate   As verbs, both mean *move part of the body, usually hands or arms, to express or emphasise an idea.* *Gesticulate* is the more normal word if gestures are of an excited nature and if communication is made in signs only (e.g. waving to attract attention). *Gesture* exists also as a noun.

gibe, gybe, jibe   *Gibe* is another word for *taunt, jeer* (noun and verb). *Gybe* is a nautical term (noun and verb) describing the action of a sail in moving from side to side on a vessel or of a ship changing course so that the sail does this. *Jibe* is an alternative spelling to both of these words.

gigantic: see **gargantuan**.

gipsy, gypsy   Alternative spellings. *Gypsy* is the older and better, *gipsy* the more common. The modern tendency is to use *traveller* because of the pejorative or even racist associations that *gypsy* is felt to have.

glance, glimpse   The difference is that between a look and a view. Both are brief, but a *glance* is sufficient to see or show what one wishes to see or show whereas a *glimpse* is fleeting and incomplete, sometimes in difficult circumstances. A *glance* may be given (*cast a glance over it*) or received (*her glance thrilled him*); a *glimpse* may only be received (*caught a glimpse of the summit through a gap in the mist*).
Both words are also verbs having the same distinctions.

glower, lower, lour   *Glower* means *stare or look scowling or angry*. *Lower* (of which *lour* is the alternative spelling) may be used to mean exactly the same, but it is normally used of a threatening sky to mean *indicate that bad weather is on the way*. *Glower* cannot be used in this sense.
All three verbs rhyme with *flower* and have the adjectival forms *glowering, lowering* and *louring*.

goodbye, bye-bye: see **bi-**.

gorilla, guer(r)illa   *Gorilla* is the animal, *guer(r)illa* the soldier.

gourmand, gourmet   These need to be distinguished. A *gourmand* is a person who enjoys hearty eating and is inclined to greed. A *gourmet* is a connoisseur of food who eats with discrimination.
The first syllable of both rhymes with *poor*. The *-mand* is pronounced *m'nd*, and the *-met* as *may*. To pronounce *gourmand* with the

final syllable nazalised as *mon* in French is an affectation, the word having been in the English language since well before Shakespeare's time.

graceful, gracious
> *graceful*: beautiful in form, style or action.
> *gracious*: kind and courteous; characteristic of an elegant and wealthy style of living.

In some contexts *gracious* may carry the implication (perhaps ironical or disparaging) that kindly indulgence is being shown towards an inferior.

graffito, graffiti   The second is the plural of the first. Strictly speaking, a piece of scribbling on a lavatory wall is a *graffito*, and several constitute *graffiti*. But *graffiti* is in common use as a singular, and *graffito* is seldom used. Only a pedant would object to *Graffiti is a curse of our time*.

grandiloquent: see **magniloquent**.

grateful, gratified   There is obviously some overlap, but also a distinction:
> *grateful*:   feeling thankful.
> *gratified*:   feeling pleased, satisfied, indulged.

grey, gray   *Gray* is acceptable as a variant spelling of *grey* but it is now seldom found outside American English, where it is customary.

griffin, griffon   A *griffin* (sometimes spelt *gryphon* or *griffon*) is a mythological winged monster with an eagle's head and lion's body. A *griffon* is a type of dog or vulture.

grill, grille   As nouns, *grill* is the cookery term and *grille* the word for a framework of bars used as a partition, screen or grating (*the radiator grille* on a car). There are signs that *grille* is being gradually superseded by *grill*, which is an acceptable alternative spelling.

grisly, grizzly, grizzled
> *grisly*:   inspiring feelings of horror or disgust.
> *grizzly*:   a kind of bear. Also a variant of *grizzled*.
> *grizzled*:   streaked with grey; having grey hair.

Grisly is pronounced like *grizzly*.

groin, groyn   *Groin* is the part of the body, *groyne* the wall or jetty built out from a shore, usually to prevent erosion. *Groyne* is spelt *groin* in American English.

gross: see **crass**.

groyne: see **groin**.

grudge: see **begrudge**.

guarantee, guaranty, guarantor, warranty   *Guaranty* is a little-used and unnecessary word as its meaning is one of those of *guarantee*: a pledge to accept responsibility for another's obligations if he defaults. A *guarantee* is also a general promise, or a particular assurance, normally in writing, that a product will meet stated standards, usually for a stated period, and that it will be replaced or repaired if it does not. A *guarantor* is a person who offers a *guarantee* (*or guaranty*). A *warranty*, in its popular sense, is a written pledge of the quality of goods with a promise to make good any defects during a given period. In this sense it merely duplicates one of those of *guarantee*.

Only *guarantee* will do in the general sense of *something that makes an outcome certain*, as in *Money is no guarantee of happiness*.

guer(r)illa: see **gorilla**.

gybe: see **gibe**.

gypsy: see **gipsy**.

H

hail, hale

hail (verb):	greet; acclaim; call out to (*He was hailed as a hero; to hail a taxi*).
hale (verb):	drag (*He was haled before the court*).
hail (noun):	frozen rain (also verb); bombardment of missiles, words, abuse, etc. (also verb).
hale (adjective):	healthy.

handicraft, handiwork   The first is manual skill, the second work done by hands. *Handicraft* can also be an occupation needing manual skill or, more frequently, products made by craft (e.g. in woodwork, pottery or sewing). The products of *handiwork* may require skill (*That wall is my handiwork*) but the word is also used more generally for any work, or even actions, done personally, including actions with an unsatisfactory outcome (*The breakdown in pay negotiations is the employers' handiwork*). *Handicraft* cannot be used in this sense, and (unlike *handiwork*) always requires skill.

hangar, hanger   The first is for aircraft, the other for clothes.

hanged, hung   Only people are *hanged*, either on the gallows or in slang expressions such as *I'll be hanged if I will*, meaning *I won't*. Things, such as pictures or parliaments, are *hung*.

hanger: see **hangar**.

hara-kiri, kamikaze   Both are forms of Japanese suicide, *hara-kiri* (or *harakiri*) by slitting one's belly, *kamikaze* by crashing one's aircraft on the enemy. The mispronunciation *hari-kari* is so frequent that the corresponding spelling is now beginning to find its way into dictionaries as a standard form.

   Hara-kiri is a noun (*to commit hara-kiri*) and *kamikaze* is usually used as an adjective (*a kamikaze pilot*). Both may be used figuratively: a government's *kamikaze policies* are ones likely to destroy the government itself – an example of committing *political hara-kiri*.

harbinger, messenger   A *harbinger* is a precursor – a person or thing announcing or foreshadowing the approach of someone or something, as certain sorts of flowers may be described as *the harbingers of spring*. A harbinger may bring something, but a *messenger* brings or announces only messages.

hari-kari: see **hara-kiri**.

haste, hasten   *Haste* is the noun (*make haste*) and *hasten* the verb (*I hasten to say*). Some dictionaries admit *haste* as a verb, others describe it as old-fashioned or poetic.

heel over, keel over   *Heel over* (tilt to one side) is applied to things, usually moving ones (e.g. a ship in a storm or a lorry with an uneven load). *Keel over* means *turn upside down* when used of ships, and *collapse*, *faint* when used of people.

heritage, inheritance   The *heri* in both relates to *heir*, and both refer to something handed down from a preceding person or time. *Inheritance* is the more general and neutral word, denoting anything from a single physical object inherited by one person to large, abstract attributes which a whole nation has acquired from its tradition. *Heritage* is restricted to the latter rather grand sense, and always signifies something important, piously regarded, and of national importance (our *cultural* heritage).

hesitancy, hesitation Generally interchangeable. *Hesitation* is the more common word, relating to *hesitate*. *Hesitancy* relates to *hesitant* and has more to do with a characteristic tendency to hesitate than with the act of hesitation. In other words, *the prime minister's hesitancy* suggests a proneness whereas *the prime minister's hesitation* indicates an act not necessarily characteristic.

Hindi, Hindu A *Hindu* is a person whose religion is Hinduism. *Hindi* is a language of northern India.

historic, historical

> *historic*: noted in history; deserving to be noted in history; significant, important (*tomorrow's historic meeting*).
>
> *historical*: belonging or pertaining to history or its study (*historical research/novel/events*).

Normal pronunciation requires that the *h* is pronounced and the words preceded by *a*, not *an*. A dropped *h* preceded by *an* is old-fashioned or pedantic or sloppy.

histrionics, hysterics Both are forms of wild, exaggerated behaviour, especially in the content or manner of speech.

> *histrionics*: flamboyant, theatrical behaviour; emotional speech or actions meant insincerely or for effect only.
>
> *hysterics*: frantic behaviour, often with screaming or unrestrained weeping and uncontrolled physical movement.

The first are assumed; the second result from loss of control.

In colloquial speech *hysterics* is sometimes used, by way of exaggeration, of behaviour that is no more than over-excited.

hoard, horde The two are frequently confused.

> *hoard*: stock, store (often valuable or hidden away).
>
> *horde*: crowd, gang (of people or insects).

Both rhyme with *ford*.

homonym, homophone Everyone agrees that a *homophone* is a word which is pronounced in the same way as another word but which has a different meaning or spelling or both (e.g. *horde*, *hoard*). There is no such unanimity about *homonym*. Some dictionaries give it the same definition as *homophone*; most regard it as a word with the same sound and spelling as another, but again with a different meaning (e.g. *mole* – animal/pier/pigmented spot on skin, etc.).

honorary, honourable
> *honorary*: given as an honour (*honorary degree* i.e. one that is not worked for in the normal way but conferred out of respect); unpaid (*honorary treasurer*).
>
> *honourable*: worthy of honour; showing honour (*an honourable defeat*).

The different spelling of the second syllables is to be noted.

hoodoo, voodoo   A *hoodoo* is merely bad luck, or the person or thing that causes it. *Voodoo*, being a type of witchcraft, is much more sinister.

horde: see **hoard**.

human, humane   As an adjective, *human* is generally a neutral term meaning *characteristic of human beings* (hence *human nature, human error*) though it is sometimes used to imply a characteristic held to be good (*Despite his austere appearance he is really very human*, i.e. approachable, sympathetic, etc.). In that sense it approaches the meaning of *humane* which is specifically *showing compassion*.

The opposites are *inhuman* (lacking all human qualities) and *inhumane* (lacking compassion), the first being the more general and severe term.

humanist, humanitarian   The first has specialist meanings in literature and philosophy, but in everyday language a *humanist* is a person who believes in and asserts the worth and interests of man, rejecting the supernatural. A *humanitarian* is more specifically concerned to promote human welfare (and may, of course, act from spiritual motives).

humour: see **wit**.

hung: see **hanged**.

hyphenate, hyphen   *Hyphenate* is an unnecessary form: little or no confusion is likely to be caused by the use of *hyphen* as a verb as well as a noun. So, *non-essential* is hyphened, an example of hyphening, and it is a waste of ink to regard it as hyphenated and an example of hyphenation.

hypocritical, hypercritical

> *hypocritical*: pretending to have virtues one does not have or beliefs one does not genuinely hold.
>
> *hypercritical*: very or too much given to criticise.

The prefix *hyper-* generally denotes excess or abnormal excess (*hyperactive*, *hypersensitive*, etc.).

hysterics: see **histrionics**.

I

ideal, idealistic

> *ideal*: perfect.
>
> *idealistic*: pursuing perfection, believing that people and things can be (made) perfect or near-perfect compared with what they are.

Ideal is normally applied to things (*ideal home*) and less frequently to people (*an ideal candidate*); *idealistic* is normally applied to people or their activities (*idealistic thinking*).

illegal, unlawful, illicit, illegitimate   Anything *illegal* is contrary to the law of the land. *Unlawful*, a slightly more formal term, has the same meaning, but can also be applied to other sorts of law, such as the laws of a religion. Something that is *illicit* is not permitted, and is usually done in secret, but it is not necessarily against the law (*illicit smoking at school*). That which is *illegitimate* may be outside the law or simply not in accordance with normal practice or rules (*a low blow in boxing is illegitimate*); it may also mean *not logical* (*an illegitimate argument*).

For **illicit** see also **elicit**.

illegible, ineligible, unreadable   Both *illegible* and *unreadable* mean *impossible to read* and can be applied, for example, to a person's handwriting. Careful users of the language prefer to retain *illegible* for this meaning and to use *unreadable* for another that *illegible* does not share: impossible to read because of tedious content, turgid style or whatever.

Ineligible is quite different: it means *not qualified or suitable* as in *Children are ineligible to vote*.

illicit

illicit: see **elicit** and **illegal**.

illusion: for **delusion/illusion**, see **allusion**.

illusory: see **elusive**.

imaginary, imaginative
> *imaginary*: not real, existing in the imagination.
> *imaginative*: having a vivid imagination; produced by the (creative) imagination (*an imaginative plan*).

imbue, infuse One may *infuse* (instil, inculcate) a quality into a person, or he may be *infused* (inspired) with it, though there is some doubt as to whether one can *infuse* him with it. One may *imbue* (inspire) a person or a thing with a quality, but one cannot *imbue* a quality into a person or thing. *Imbue* is usually followed by *with*: an example of the word used correctly is *a leader/campaign imbued with patriotism* (not *he imbued patriotism into his followers/campaign*). But *he infused patriotism into . . .* is fine.
> See **instil**.

imitate: see **emulate**.

immanent: see **eminent**.

immerse, submerge To *immerse* is to dip into liquid or, figuratively, to engross (*immersed in a book*). To *submerge* is to put or go under water or to cover with water; figuratively it means *overwhelm* (*submerged in work*). Immersion is temporary (*immerse a wounded finger in antiseptic*); submersion may be temporary (but is usually deeper) or permanent (*ship hit a submerged reef*).

immigrant: see **emigrant**.

imminent: see **eminent**.

immoral: see **amoral**.

immunity, impunity
> *immunity*: freedom from obligation and especially from a specific disease; being unaffected by.
> *impunity*: freedom from punishment or unwanted consequences.
> *Impunity* is often found in the expression *with impunity*, without risk of unpleasant consequences. *Immunity* is followed by *to* when it means *unsusceptible to* (*immunity to change*) and by *from* when it means *exempt from* (*immunity from tax*).

impassive, impassioned

> *impassive*: free from passion or emotion; imperturbable (*a government impassive in the face of criticism*).
>
> *impassioned*: full of passion (*an impassioned protest*).

impel, induce

> *impel*: drive into action.
>
> *induce*: move by persuasion; bring about.

The difference is seen in *She felt impelled to complain, in the hope that this would induce others to do the same* and *She was induced to complain, and this impelled others to do the same*.

For **impel** see also **compel**.

impending: see **pending**.

imperial, imperative, imperious

> *imperial*: pertaining to empire or a sovereign.
>
> *imperative*: urgent; obligatory.
>
> *imperious*: overbearing, domineering.

Imperative is also a noun for a command or something urgent or necessary.

impinge, infringe Both mean *encroach*, so that one may *infringe* or *impinge on* someone's privacy. The senses are slightly different, however, because *infringe* has the additional meaning of *violate* (a rule): infringing therefore implies serious or even deliberate disregard of propriety, whereas *impinge* merely has the sense of *have an effect on*, the implication being that impinging on someone's privacy may be less significant or even inadvertent.

implication: see **imply**.

implicit: see **explicit**.

imply, infer Getting these the wrong way round is one of the commonest errors.

> *imply*: express indirectly.
>
> *infer*: deduce.

A speaker implies; a hearer infers something from what the speaker says (or perhaps from what he implies). The corresponding nouns are *implication* (implied significance) and *inference* (inferred conclusion).

There is nothing indirect, hinting, unstated (i.e. implied) in *infer* and *inference*, both of which depend on a logical process of drawing a conclusion from evidence.

The common error is for someone to say *He inferred that . . .* when he means *He implied that . . . .*

impracticable, impractical, unpractical   There is general agreement about *impracticable* (incapable of being put into practice). There is some controversy over *impractical*, which some authorities insist means the same as *impracticable* and others prefer to define as *not worth putting into practice*, i.e. practicable in theory but not in reality (because too complicated, expensive, etc.). However, all agree that *impractical* also means, when applied to people, *not good at doing things. Unpractical* is an alternative to *impractical* in this sense.

A reasonably safe course is to use *impracticable* for *unworkable* (whether in theory or reality) and *impractical* (or *unpractical*) for *not skilful in practical matters*.

impromptu: see **extempore**.

impulsive: see **compulsory**.

impunity: see **immunity**.

inability, disability
> *inability*:   lack of power, means or capacity (*inability to pay*).
> *disability*:   handicap, lack of ability because of physical or mental defect.

See also **unable**.

inapt, inept   Both mean *unsuitable*, but something or somebody *inapt* is inappropriate by reason of lack of ability or capacity and *inept* by reason of being out of place, clumsy or absurd. *Inept* also means *unskilful*.

incapable: see **unable**.

incapacitated: see **disabled**.

inchoate, incoherent, chaotic
> *inchoate*:   only begun, unfinished; imperfectly formulated; unformed.
> *incoherent*:   unintelligible, loose, rambling.
> *chaotic*:   in disorder.

Inchoate is normally applied to thoughts and feelings. Its first two syllables are pronounced as in *incoherent* but with the stress on the second syllable. It does not mean the same as *incoherent*, however.

incidental: see **accidental**.

incite: see **excite**.

incoherent: see **inchoate**.

incomparable: see **comparable**.

incongruous: see **ironic**.

inconsequential, inconsequent   Both mean *irrelevant, inconsequential* in the sense of *without importance, inconsequent* in the sense of *not following logically.*
   See **consequent**.

increase: see **maximise**.

incredible: see **credible**.

incredulous: see **credible**.

incubus, succubus   The first is a male, the second a female demon, both prone to fornication with sleeping humans. They are more familiar in their figurative use, as some man or woman who oppresses one like a nightmare. An *incubus* may also be a *thing* that has the burdensome qualities of a bad dream.

inculcate, indoctrinate   The notion of teaching is common to both, but:
   inculcate: impress something (on person) by persistent repetition.
   indoctrinate: cause person to accept a system of thought, usually partisan.
   One inculcates (but does not indoctrinate) ideas into people, and indoctrinates (but does not inculcate) people. It is wrong to say *People were inculcated with . . . .* See **instil** for the correct alternative.

inculpate, inculcate
   inculpate: accuse, involve in a charge (*The evidence inculpated three men*).
   For *inculcate*, see previous entry.

incumbent, recumbent
   incumbent: pressing or resting on one as a duty (*It is incumbent on you to . . .*).
   recumbent: lying down, reclining.

indefensible

Recumbent is only an adjective. *Incumbent* may be used as a noun denoting the holder of an office, especially an ecclesiastical benefice.

indefensible: see **defensible**.

indifferent, diffident   As well as being similar in sound, both denote lack of assertiveness. *Indifferent* means *not caring about something* or even *off-hand*: *diffident* means *lacking in confidence*. The first is likely to be used of someone's action, the second of manner or temperament.
   Indifferent also means *mediocre*, as in *an indifferent meal*.

indiscriminate, undiscriminating   The sense of not making careful distinctions is common to both. However, *indiscriminate* means *confused, reckless, random, careless*, as in *the indiscriminate use of exclamation marks. Undiscriminating* is applied to judgement or taste and means *not judicious, showing lack of discernment. Indiscriminate* is not so limited: *indiscriminate firing/punishment/drinking*, etc.
   See **discriminating**.

indoctrinate: see **inculcate**.

indoor, indoors   *Indoor* is the adjective meaning *belonging to or done inside a building* (*indoor sport*). *Indoors* is the adverb meaning *in or into a building* and is normally used of human activity (*went indoors because it started to snow*) but in Cockney usage it means *at home* and can be used of things (*got to the restaurant and discovered he'd left his false teeth indoors*).

indorse: see **endorse**.

indubitable: see **redoubtable**.

induce: see **impel** and **induct**.

inducement: see **induction**.

induct, induce   Apart from various scientific and medical applications, *induce* means *persuade*. *Induct* means *initiate* (a person), often with ceremony. The corresponding nouns are *inducement* and *induction*.
   See **deduce, induction**.

induction, deduction, inducement   The first two have a number of meanings, but the ones most likely to be confused are those connected with methods of reasoning. *Induction* is arguing from particular facts to draw a general principle. *Deduction* is the reverse: assuming the truth of a particular fact from the existence of a general principle.

For example, from observing some careless foreign drivers you might assume by induction that all foreign drivers are careless as a general principle. Conversely, if you had been led to believe as a generalisation that all foreign drivers are careless, you may be led by deduction to the conclusion that the next foreign driver you encounter will be a menace, even though you have no idea who he will be.

Inducement is quite different: it is the act or means of persuading, attracting, influencing or bringing about.

See **induct** and **adduce**.

industrious, industrial
> *industrious*: hardworking, constantly working.
> *industrial*: related to productive industry (*industrial development*); having such industries (*industrial nations*).

inedible: see **eatable**.

ineligible: see **illegible**.

inept: see **inapt**.

inequitable, iniquitous
> *inequitable*: unfair.
> *iniquitous*: wicked.

In certain contexts, *iniquitous* may carry the sense of *wicked because unjust*.

inessential: see **non-essential**.

inexplicable: see **unexplained**.

infamous: see **notorious**.

infectious: see **contagious**.

infer: see **imply**.

inference: see **imply**.

inflammable, flammable, inflammatory   One would be forgiven for assuming that the first two are opposites, *flammable* meaning *easily set on fire* and *inflammable* meaning *not easily* .... Not so: they are synonyms having the first meaning. For this reason, warning labels normally carry the word *flammable* to avoid serious misunderstanding; the opposite is *non-flammable*. *Inflammable* is to be used with care, if at all.

Inflammatory is usually figurative, meaning *tending to inflame*, i.e. to arouse trouble, passions, etc. (*make an inflammatory speech*).

inflict: see **afflict**.

informant, informer   Both denote a person who provides information, but an *informer* provides (incriminating) information to an authority, usually the police, whereas an *informant* merely passes on information (which may be innocent, such as gossip) or knowledge. *Informer* thus has disagreeable overtones which *informant* does not have.

infringe: see **impinge**.

infuse: see **imbue** and **instil**.

ingenious, ingenuous
> *ingenious*:   resourceful, inventive, clever, original, skilful.
> *ingenuous*:   having a childlike innocence and frankness; artless; unable to dissimulate.

   Ingenuous is close to *naive,* though that word carries a tone of criticism whereas *ingenuous* implies a certain endearing quality.
   The corresponding nouns are *ingenuity* and *ingenuousness*.

inherent, innate   The sense of both is *existing as an inseparable part. Inherent* (intrinsic) is normally applied to things (*an inherent part of his work*) and *innate* (existing from birth) to people or their qualities or character (*his innate cruelty*). *Innate* also means *instinctive, not learnt*.

inheritance: see **heritage**.

inhibit, prohibit   To *inhibit* is to prevent or discourage by inner, psychological checks (or by such abstractions as social codes or expectations) whereas to *prohibit* is to prevent by the exercise of authority. They come close in some contexts – for instance, a social code may be felt to carry the weight of authority: *inhibited/prohibited from smoking by public disapproval*. But generally *prohibit* implies enforcement and *inhibit* (usually in the passive – *he was/felt inhibited by* . . .) implies restraint by something less tangible, such as one's personal feelings.

inhuman, inhumane: see **human**.

iniquitous: see **inequitable**.

innate: see **inherent**.

innocuous, innocent   The meaning of *innocuous* (not harmful, inoffensive) is shared by *innocent* (*an innocuous/innocent conversation/game/*

person, etc.) though *innocuous* is more likely to be used in this sense, leaving *innocent* to be used in its many other senses not shared by *innocuous*. These include *free from guilt or evil, lacking, not knowing, artless* and *simple-minded*.

innuendo: see **insinuation**.

innumerable: see **numerous**.

inquire: see **enquire**.

inquiry: see **enquiry** and **query**.

insensate, insensible, insensitive Although both of the first two mean *lacking sensation or consciousness, insensate* is normally used to mean *unfeeling, without delicacy*, or even *senseless, mad. Insensible* also means *unaware of* or *indifferent to* (usually after a verb and followed by *to*: *he seems insensible to pain*) or *callous*. It is occasionally used in the sense of *imperceptible*.

Insensitive can also mean *lacking sensation* but the familar meaning is *not aware or responsive* (especially with regard to the feelings of others), *not registering differences or subtleties*.

See **sensible**.

insidious: see **invidious**.

insinuation, innuendo A hint of an indirect and usually unpleasant kind may be called by either word, but one normally speaks of *the/an insinuation* as a single hint and of *innuendo* as a technique or the creation of an impression (*statement/jokes full of innuendo; he works by innuendo*).

insoluble: see **unsolvable**.

insolvable: see **unsolvable**.

instantly, instantaneously, simultaneously The distinction between the first two is fine: *instantly* is *at once* and *instantaneously* is *within an instant*. In some contexts, therefore, it is immaterial which is used. *Simultaneously* means *at the same time* and implies . . . *as something else*. Thus *He came instantly* (immediately), *He died instantaneously* (within an instant), *They arrived simultaneously* (at the same time as each other).

instil, imbue *Instil* means *infuse slowly* (as if drop by drop), *impart gradually, implant* or *cause* (something) *to permeate*. One may *instil* something, such as an idea or quality, *into* a person's mind or feelings (*education should instil a sense of curiosity into pupils*). One cannot *instil* a person *with* something. Conversely, one may *imbue* (inspire) a person or thing *with* a quality (*she imbued her home/family with a sense of fun*) but not *imbue* something *into* someone or something. Those dictionaries that give *instil* and *imbue* as synonyms are merely recording sloppy usage.

The whole problem of these and other *in-* words having to do with impressing people with things or things in people may be summarised:

instil/inculcate/infuse thing *into* person.

imbue/inspire person (or thing) *with* something.

See **imbue, inculcate**.

instinctively, intuitively   Instinct is the natural impulse to do something (especially to respond to a stimulus) without needing to think and without conscious intention. Intuition is immediate perception by the mind without any evident process of thinking, deduction or analysis. *Instinctively* therefore means *by natural impulse* and *intuitively by direct apprehension*. Careful writers will observe this distinction between a physical process and a mental one (*instinctively felt danger* but not *instinctively knew; intuitively realised* but not *recoiled intuitively*) though there are contexts when either word will serve — *distrusted him instinctively* (i.e. by the operation of feelings) or *distrusted him intuitively* (i.e. by knowing he was not to be trusted).

institution, institute   Marriage, parliament, family life and universities are all examples of an *institution* — an established custom or practice in society, or an established organisation, usually a cultural or charitable one. *Institute* is restricted to a foundation or organisation devoted to education or public work, or to the building that houses it, though some old-established organisations have *institution* in their title in this sense.

instructional, instructive   Both of these adjectives have to do with the imparting of knowledge. *Instructional* is the more neutral term, meaning *intending to provide instruction or information*: an *instructional film* is different from one designed to provide amusement or tell a story. *Instructive* means *tending* (rather than *intending*) *to instruct*: the emphasis is on the learning, not the intention to furnish it. A person who has learnt from an experience has had an instructive one, though it may not have been intended to be instructional.

insurance: see **assurance**.

insure: see **assure**.

intellect, intelligence   *Intelligence* is the general word for the mind and the ability to use it. *Intellect* means the same, but tends to be used more specifically of a highly competent mind, good at scholarship and abstract thoughts and understanding. One would, for example, refer to an animal's *intelligence* rather than *intellect*. *Intelligence* also implies more of an emphasis on the practical, quick or inventive applications of mental prowess whereas *intellect* applies to the prowess itself.

Intelligence sometimes means *news* or information.

See **intellectual**.

intellectual, intelligent, intelligible   The distinction between the first two adjectives is sharper than that between the corresponding nouns (see **intellect**). *Intellectual* means not only *showing intellect* (rather than feelings) but also *concerned with things of the mind*. A person who is *intelligent* has a sharp mind, but may have no interest in intellectual matters (e.g. scholarship, academic speculation) whereas an *intellectual* person is intelligent by definition. Clever people have *intelligent conversation*, but *intellectual conversation* is about scholarly concerns.

Intelligible means *capable of being understood*, usually by the mind rather than the senses.

intense, intensive   The differences are more in usage than in meaning. *Intense* (extreme in quality or degree) is the more common word, applied to what is felt (*intense cold/sadness/hunger/dislike*) or shown (*intense concentration/care/effort*). It also means *very serious in feelings* (*an intense person/conversation/argument*). *Intensive* (employing much effort) is applied to undertakings (*intensive enquiries/training/course of study*) and to the application of resources in a concentrated way (*intensive care* in hospital; an industry that is *labour-intensive; intensive farming*).

See **extensive** and **intently**.

intentionally: see **advisedly**.

intently, intensely   Easily confused because if you look at something *intently* you will do so with *intense* concentration.

> *intently*:   earnestly, eagerly, with close attention.
>
> *intensely*: extremely; ardently.

The first is usually found on its own (*to listen intently*); the second may be on its own (*to dislike intensely*) or before an adjective (*It was intensely interesting*).

inter, intern

> *inter*:   bury.

> *intern*: confine within prescribed limits (especially prisoners of war or enemy aliens during wartime).

The corresponding nouns are *interment* and *internment*.

interject, interpolate, interpose All mean *introduce* (e.g. a comment, question) *into a conversation or someone's speech*. *Interpose* is probably the most common word, and can also mean *intervene* (using oneself or one's influence) *to alter a situation*, or *place something between other things*, as a composer may interpose a slow passage between two quick ones. *Interject* has a rather sharp ring about it, suggesting (when correctly used) abrupt interruption, but it is often used to mean no more than *have one's say*; it can also mean *remark parenthetically*. *Interpolate* can mean *falsify* (e.g. a document) by making additions, but it is generally used to mean *intervene* (vocally), *interrupt* or *insert* (remark, etc.) by way of intervention or interruption.

intern, internment: see **inter**.

interpolate: see **interject**.

interpose: see **interject**.

interrogate, question To *interrogate* is to cross-examine, to question formally and often sternly, and face to face. One may *question* a person (in all these ways, but in others too) and also a thing, such as a belief, assertion or written statement, but one may *interrogate* only a person.

interrogative, interrogatory Used mainly as a grammatical term, *interrogative* is a noun (*question*) and adjective (*questioning*). It is in this latter sense that it is most commonly found (*an interrogative tone of voice*). *Interrogatory* is little used: it means *expressing a question*, though it has a flavour of interrogating rather than questioning.

See **interrogate**.

into, in to Two words are needed when *in* is an adverb describing a preceding verb and *to* is part of an infinitive (*went in to rest*) or a preposition introducing what follows (*went in to his wife*). *Into* is a preposition (*went into great detail*). *In to* denotes that the two words have separate force and function.

intolerant, intolerable

> *intolerant*:   not tolerant; unable to treat the actions (beliefs, etc.) of others with forbearance.
>
> *intolerable*:   not tolerable; unacceptable; not to be endured.

intrusive: see **obtrusive**.

intuitively: see **instinctively**.

invaluable, valueless   One might think that *invaluable* is the opposite of *valuable*, as *incoherent* is the opposite of *coherent*. Not so: *invaluable* is the opposite of *valueless*. They mean *having great value* and *having no value* respectively.

inveigh, inveigle   Despite similarities in appearance and sound (they are pronounced *in-vay* and *in-vay-gl*, with the stress on the second syllable) these two are quite different in meaning. To *inveigh* is to denounce, accuse or protest with violence or bitter abuse, and is followed by *against*: it is related to *invective*. To *inveigle* is to persuade (someone to do something), obtain (something) or lead (someone into something) by cleverness, trickery or cajolery (*inveigled one into investing money; inveigled his way out of the problem*).

inverse: see **contrary**.

invidious, insidious
    invidious: likely to cause offence (by being or appearing to be unjust).
    insidious: progressing or spreading harmfully in a subtle way (*insidious rumour*).
    Invidious often occurs in the expression *it would be invidious* (unfair, unfortunate) *to* . . . .

inward, inwards   *Inwards* is the adverb (*the doors open inwards*) and *inward* usually the adjective (*inward peace*), but it is quite acceptable to use *inward* adverbially.

ironic, incongruous, ironical   The essence of irony is that it is a use of words to mean the *opposite* of what they normally mean, e.g. *That WAS clever* meaning *That was foolish*. An *ironic* state of affairs is the *opposite* of (or at least very different from) what was intended or expected, in a way that seems to mock those having the expectations or intentions. There is no good reason to weaken this special meaning of *ironic* by using the word as a mere substitute for *incongruous* (inappropriate), *odd, unexpected*, etc., as often happens.
    Ironical means the same as *ironic*.
    See **sarcastic**.

irreparable: see **repairable**.

irreproachable, unapproachable
> *irreproachable*: beyond reproach; without fault.
> *unapproachable*: impossible or difficult to approach; unfriendly.

irritate: see **aggravate**.

irrupt: see **erupt**.

Islamic: see **Moslem**.

iterate: see **reiterate**.

its, it's Two commonly confused words: *its* means *belonging to it* but *it's* is an abbreviation for *it is*.

J

jail: see **gaol**.

jejune, juvenile An unfamiliar word, *jejune* (pronounced *ji-joon* with the stress on the second syllable) means *insipid, unsatisfying, dull, lacking interest* and is often applied to works of art and to human expression (e.g. argument, point of view). It has come to mean *immature, naive, puerile, unsophisticated*, and applied to behaviour or taste, though some would regard this as incorrect usage.

Juvenile as a noun is the technical word for a child or young person below a legally defined age (*juvenile court, juvenile delinquent*). As an adjective it means *having to do with a child or young person* and is usually a disparaging word for *immature* (*juvenile behaviour by MPs in parliament*). See **juvenile**.

jetsam: see **flotsam**.

jibe: see **gibe**.

joky, jocular, jovial, jocose, joking
> *joky*: inclined to joke. (Applied to person or thing, e.g. book.) Also *jokey*.
> *jocular*: habitually jolly; of a humorous nature or intention (*has a jocular manner*).
> *jovial*: convivial, hearty, good-humoured. (Applied to person or his behaviour.)
> *jocose*: playful, light-hearted. (Rare and rather literary.)
> *joking*: not serious, for fun. (Applied to things (*in a joking way*).)

judicial, judicious
>*judicial*:   relating to a court of law, a judge or a judgement.
>*judicious*: sensible, prudent.
>*Judicial* is normally a legal word, *judicious* a general one.

junction, juncture   These have limited uses. *Juncture* is hardly ever encountered except in the phrase *at this juncture*, an elaborate way of saying *now*. *Junction* (a place where things come together) is used of roads, railway lines, electric wires, pipework and the like. In figurative uses, *conjunction* is needed.

juvenile, puerile   Both may be terms of abuse meaning *immature*, but as *juvenile* is associated with youth and *puerile* with childhood, *puerile* is the more extreme.
>See **jejune.**

K

kamikaze: see **hara-kiri.**

keel over: see **heel over.**

kerb: see **curb.**

kinky, quirky   Oddity is common to both. *Kinky* means *idiosyncratic, bizarre, weird*, and has strong overtones of sexual perversion. *Quirky* comes from *quirk*, a pecularity of character, a foible or eccentricity, or a sudden twist or turn (*a quirk of fate*); the adjective is usually applied to human behaviour (*a quirky sense of humour* is an unusual, slightly twisted one).

kneeled, knelt   Either will do, *knelt* being the more popular.

L

laden, loaded   In their sense of *carrying a load*, the adjective *laden* implies being oppressed by a heavy burden whereas *loaded* (part of the verb *load*) can also mean simply *filled up with a load*. Thus *a fully laden ship* will be low in the water: *a fully loaded* one may just be carrying its normal complement.

laggard, sluggard

Loaded has many other meanings, such as *biased* (*a loaded question*), *wealthy, charged with ammunition*, etc. *Laden* is not much used.

laggard, sluggard   *Sluggish* is *slow-moving*, literally (*a sluggish river*) or figuratively (*a sluggish market*). A *sluggard* is a person who is sluggish, i.e. lazy. A *laggard* is a person who lags behind or weakens (in effort, etc.).

lama, llama   Not much used, but it is just as well to get them right, a *lama* being a Buddhist monk from Tibet and a *llama* being a South American animal of the camel family.

languid, languorous
> *languid*:   apathetic; drooping; without energy, spirit, force, interest, quickness or enthusiasm; listless, sluggish (see **laggard**).
>
> *languorous*:   (of person) physically or mentally lazy, weak or tired; (of person or thing) having a feeling of dreaminess, wistfulness or relaxation; slow or still in a soporific way.

Both have a rather negative feel but can have a more positive one, *languid* in the sense of *pleasantly relaxed* and *languorous* in the sense of *gracefully slow*.

lapse, elapse   *Elapse* is used only of a period of time and means *pass by*. *Lapse* has several meanings: (of people) err; (of things) fall into disuse (*insurance policy has not been renewed and therefore lapses*); fall (back) from or fail to maintain a standard (*he lapsed into his old habits*); decline gradually (*lapsed into torpor*).
As a noun, *lapse* covers the meanings of both verbs.

larva, lava   The first is produced by an insect, the second by a volcano.

lascivious, licentious   The more general word is *licentious*: it means *unrestrained* (i.e. with licence) and can refer to any immoral behaviour but more particularly to lack of sexual restraint.
Lascivious is specifically *lustful, lecherous, lewd*.

last: see **latter**.

lath, lathe
> *lath*:   narrow strip of wood.
> *lathe*:   machine-tool for shaping wood or metal.

latter, last   The *latter* is the second of two only, normally contrasted with *former* but capable of being used without explicit comparison: *the latter part of the meeting* is the period towards the end of it. *Last (last-named)* refers to the final one of more than two. Thus *Of the two, I prefer the latter* but *Of the three, I prefer the last.*

latterly, lately   Both mean *recently*, but *latterly* is a shade formal; it can also mean (as *lately* cannot) *towards the end of a period*, though this is an uncommon usage.

laudable, laudatory
>   *laudable*:   deserving praise; commendable.
>   *laudatory*:   giving praise (*a laudatory speech*).

In some contexts *laudable* contains a hint of reservation as if anticipating the word *but*: *His intervention, though laudable, never stood much chance of succeeding.*

lava: see **larva.**

lawful, legal   *Lawful* (allowed by law) is a rather formal term, not much used outside a few standard expressions: it can be used of religious law as well as of the law of the land. *Legal* means *having to do with the law* (*the legal profession*) or authorised by law (*the legal speed-limit*) and is much the more common of the two words.
      See **illegal.**

lay: see **lie.**

lead, led   When pronounced to rhyme with *head*, *lead* is the heavy metal. Rhyming with *heed*, it is a verb of which the past tense and past participle is *led* (*He led/had led several expeditions*).

leaned, leant   Either will do as the past tense and past participle of *lean*, as in *We (had) leaned/leant over backwards to . . . Leant* is probably the more common nowadays.
      Leant must be distinguished from its homophone *lent*, which is a part of the verb *lend.*

leaped, leapt   The past tense and past participle of *leap* may be either *leaped* or *leapt*, the latter being the more common in speech, the former still persisting in writing. Both are acceptable.

learn, teach   It is a solecism to use *learn* instead of *teach* in *That will learn*

learned, learnt

him a lesson. One may teach a person or a lesson, or learn a lesson, but not learn a person.

See **learned**.

learned, learnt   Both are acceptable as the past tense or past participle of *learn*, as in *We (had) learned/learnt the news from the radio. Learnt* is probably the more common.

Learned can also mean *having or containing great knowledge.* In this sense it is pronounced as two syllables.

See **learn**.

least: see **less**

led: see **lead**.

legible: see **readable**.

leisured, leisurely   *Leisured* (having (ample) leisure) is an adjective normally applied to people who do no work, though it can be used more generally. *Leisurely* means *unhurried* (*went for a leisurely walk*) and is also an adverb (*walked leisurely*, i.e. slowly).

lend: see **loan**.

lenience, leniency, lenity   The first two are alternative spellings, *lenience* being the more common. Both mean *tolerance, mildness* or *absence of severity* in behaviour or attitude towards a person who perhaps deserved none of them. *Lenity* is a less familiar word with the more specific meaning of *mercifulness*.

lent: see **leaned**.

less, fewer, least, fewest   Use *less* for quantity and *fewer* for number. Or remember *less* + singular noun and *fewer* + plural (*Less tax, fewer taxes; less chance, fewer chances*) even though *less* is so widely used in place of *fewer* (*They have scored less goals than any other team*) that *fewer* sometimes seems in danger of dropping out of the language altogether.

Least follows the same rule as *less* in taking a singular noun: *the least chance. Fewest* takes a plural: *the fewest mistakes.*

See **less, lesser**.

less, lesser   As an adjective, *less* (smaller in amount or extent; lower in rank) can be used immediately before a singular noun and only a singular noun (*less sugar*). *Lesser* (not as great in value, quantity or size) is needed immediately before a plural noun (*was not tempted, as lesser men might have been, to . . .*).

Another restriction on *less* when it immediately precedes a noun is that it cannot itself be preceded by *a*. *Lesser* can: *he was moved to a lesser post*. *A less post* is unidiomatic, though *he was given less power* or *a lower post* is authentic.

Less may, of course, be preceded by *a* when it is an adverb: *a less prominent position*.

Lesser as an adjective may be used only immediately before a noun (*a lesser poet*). As an adverb it is usually found hyphened with part of a verb (*a lesser-known poet*). It also figures in a few stock expressions (*the lesser of two evils*).

Less is related to *little* (it means *more little*) and should not be used to mean *more small*. We refer to *a small price*, not *a little price*; we must therefore say *a smaller price*, not *a less price*. But we say *at small cost* or *at little cost*; that being so, *at less cost* (but not *a less cost*) is correct.

Lesser too is related to *little*; it is the opposite of *greater*.

See **less, fewer**.

liable: see **likely**.

libel, slander   Defamation in writing (or pictorially) used to be called *libel*; if spoken it was *slander*. This legal distinction no longer exists, and *libel* does duty for both offences, but it remains incorrect to use *slander* of a published defamation.

liberal, liberated   Politics apart, *liberal* means *generous* or *broad-minded*. *Liberated* means *freed* (from constraint or subjugation).

libertarian, libertine   A *libertarian* believes in freedom of thought and expression and in the doctrine of free will. A *libertine* is morally dissolute, especially in sexual matters.

licence, license   *Licence* is the noun, *license* the verb. American English sensibly has one spelling (the second) for both.

For advice on distinguishing between the *-ce* and *-se* spelling, see **practice**.

licentious: see **lascivious**.

lie, lay   Difficulties are caused by the various forms of these verbs rather than by their meanings.

111

lifelong, livelong

Lie (as in *lie down*) has *lying*, the past tense *lay*, and the past participle *lain* (*The ships have lain idle since the strike began*).

Lie (meaning *tell an untruth*) has *lying*, the past tense *lied*, and the past participle *lied*.

Lay (as in *lay the table*) has *laying*, the past tense *laid*, and the past participle *laid* (*I would have laid my life on it*).

The irregularity of *lie* (*down*) is the main problem, resulting in such confusions as *He has been laying in bed* or *I have laid awake all night*.

lifelong, livelong

lifelong: lasting a lifetime (*a lifelong friendship*).

livelong: entire.

Livelong is found only in the expression *the livelong day*.

lighted, lit   The past forms of the verb *light* are either *lighted* or *lit*: *I (have) lighted/lit a fire in the garden. Lit* is the usual form.

As an adjective before a noun, *lighted* is usual on its own (*a lighted match*) and *lit* when there is a preceding adverb (*a well-lit road*).

lightening, lightning   What often goes with thunder is *lightning*, also used as an adjective meaning *very rapid, short* or *sudden* (*a lightning decision*). *Lightening* is from the verb *lighten* in its sense of *make (more) light*, as in *The budget will lead to a lightening of the tax burden*. Another sense of *lighten*, possibly confusingly, is *discharge lightning*, as in *She was afraid when it began to lighten* (i.e. when lightning began).

likely, prone, apt, liable   In expressing kinds of probability (though not in other respects) these words have similarities that need to be distinguished.

likely: inclined, tending. *She is likely to win* means that it is probable she will . The word implies a specific probability, i.e. the example quoted does not imply habitual success.

prone: inclined, usually with undesirable consequences (*Prone to lose his belongings. Accident-prone*). Implies general probability.

apt: habitually inclined (but with no implication of undesirable consequences): *A horse apt to run well on firm ground*; *He is apt to cook his own breakfast*. Implies general probability.

liable: likely to suffer (always with undesirable consequences): *Liable to accidents*. Implies specific or general probability.

These usages have no bearing on other meanings of these words (*a likely story, lying prone, apt pupil, not liable for any accidents*).
See **prone**.

limit, delimit
    delimit: fix limits (*delimit the area of a building site*, i.e. determine it).
    limit: restrict by fixing limits (*limit the area of a building site* i.e. curtail it).

lineament, liniment *Liniment* is rubbed on the skin as a treatment for bruises, pain or irritation. *A lineament* is a distinctive feature or outline, usually of a face. It is normally found in the plural, and pronounced *lini-ament*.

liqueur, liquor Pronounced *lik-your* with the emphasis on the second syllable, a *liqueur* is a distilled alcoholic drink, often sweet and usually served in small measures after a meal.
    Liquor, pronounced *licker*, is any alcoholic drink or drinks, often spirits (of which *hard liquor* is sometimes used).

lit: see **lighted**.

literate, literal, literary Confusingly, *literate* can mean both *able to read and write* (*He is barely literate*) and *cultured, educated* (*an increase in the number of literate newspapers*). *Literary* is more straightforward: it means *relating to literature* as in *person with literary interests*. *Literal* is *actual, word for word* (*What he said was the literal truth*) and *having the primary or explicit meaning of an expression* (*word used in its literal sense*).

livelong: see **lifelong**.

livid, lurid
    livid: angry, furious.
    lurid: sensational; gruesome; gaudy.
    Livid can also describe skin that is discoloured (*face with a livid scar*).

llama: see **lama**.

loaded: see **laden**.

loan, lend There is something of a prejudice against the use of *loan* as a verb in the sense of *lend* (*Can you loan me your pen?*) although this is widespread (and standard in America). Some commentators find it colloquial; others describe it as unnecessary or as another example of

loath, loth, loathe

the intrusive Americanisation of the language. It is probably here to stay, though best avoided in formal writing as long as the prejudice lasts. But even its opponents accept it in the sense of *formally transfer*, as in *a valuable painting which has been loaned to the gallery* or *money loaned to the company by the bank*.

loath, loth, loathe The first two are alternatives, meaning *unwilling* or *reluctant* and rhyming with *both*. *Loth* is preferable, as its spelling distinguishes it more sharply from that of *loathe*, a verb meaning *detest* and pronounced with the *th* as in *smooth*.

location, locality, locale A *location* is a particular place where something or somebody is located. It is used particularly of an open-air site for filming, and has recently become a showy word for a factory or office site.

Locality is generally used in the sense of *district*. *Locale* is a relatively little-used word for the scene of an event, or a place associated with a specific happening.

loose, loosen, lose *Loose* is most commonly found as an adjective meaning *not tight* or *free from restraint* though it does exist as a verb meaning *release* (as in *loosed the dog*) and occasionally as a noun (*on the loose*: freed from constraint). The *s* is pronounced as in *noose*, as it is in *loosen* (to make (more) *loose*). To loose a knot is to untie it; to loosen it is to make it slacker (but still knotted). The possibility of confusion is small because *loose* is not much used as a verb: alternatives such as *undo, release, detach, set free, let fly* (*loosed their arrows*), etc. are generally preferred.

Lose, rhyming with *booze*, is the familiar word for *fail to win*, *mislay* and so on. Its pronunciation tempts some people to misspell it as *loose*.

loth: see **loath**.

lour: see **glower**.

lower: see **glower**.

lunch, luncheon *Luncheon* is very formal, and is hardly ever used except in some standard phrases such as *luncheon meat* (a mixture of meat and cereal, usually sold in tins) and *luncheon voucher* (issued to employees to be exchanged for food). The normal word is *lunch*.

lure, allure Both mean *attract*, the first implying *dangerously* or *disadvantageously*, the second *pleasantly* or *favourably*. *Allure* is normally found in its form *alluring*.

The two words are common as nouns with the same distinction.

lurid: see **livid**.

lustful, lusty Lust is any strong drive, desire or enjoyment (*lust for glory*) or, more particularly, strong sexual desire. *Lustful* has both senses: a miser or a libertine could be described as lustful for different reasons, with the implication that their desires invite condemnation, though the word is most frequently used with sexual connotations.
    Lusty is quite different: it means *full of strength or vitality* as in *lusty singing/enjoyment*, etc.

luxuriant, luxurious
    luxuriant: prolific, profuse, fertile (*a luxuriant beard*); exuberant, richly ornamented (*a luxuriant style of architecture*).
    luxurious: characterised by luxury (*a luxurious house*); voluptuous.

lyric, lyrical As an adjective, *lyric* is not much used except in reference to poetry or drama: it means *ardently expressing personal emotions or thoughts*, especially of the sort often expressed in song. *Lyrical* means *using language appropriate to lyric poetry*; more popularly it means *expressing admiration or enthusiasm* (*She was waxing lyrical about her holiday*).

M

machismo: see **sadism**.

madam, madame *Madam* is a formal term of address (*Madam Chairman, Dear Madam*). A *madam*, without an initial capital, is a female brothel-keeper and also a disparaging word sometimes applied to a pert or conceited girl (*a proper little madam*).
    Madame, apart from being the French equivalent of *Mrs*, is sometimes used in English as a courtesy title for married ladies of other nationalities. It used to be adopted – and perhaps still is – by fortune-tellers, stage performers, proprietors of dress-shops and other English ladies feeling the need of a more exotic identity.

magic, magical Two distinctions separate these generally interchangeable words. One is that *magic* is best for the specifically supernatural (*a magic carpet*) and *magical* for the more generally extraordinary (*a magical effect*). The other is that *magical* is the more normal when one of the adjectives is needed after a verb (*The transformation was magical*).

magisterial, magistral Both adjectives derive from a Latin word meaning *master*. They are normally applied to statements (judgements, opinions, rebukes, etc.) delivered authoritatively from on high, with effortless control, in a manner brooking no contradiction. *Magisterial*, the more common word, also has associations with *magistrate*, and has a flavour of *dictatorial* as well as *authoritative*. *Magistral*, an unfamiliar word, is milder and means *masterly*. Both are pronounced with a soft *g* as in *general*.

magnanimous, munificent

    magnanimous: generous and noble in spirit and conduct.

    munificent: generous in giving money.

magnate, magnet Originally a nobleman or a person of great influence or eminence in any sphere, a *magnate* is now a person of power in the management of industry. A *magnet* is a thing (occasionally a person) with the power to attract.

magniloquent, grandiloquent Boastfulness is common to both, but the distinction (if there actually is one outside dictionaries, and in some dictionaries there is not) is that *grandiloquent* expression is pompous or bombastic and *magniloquent* is lofty or ambitious.

maladroit, malapropos Unusual words, but perhaps inviting confusion because of their Frenchness.

    maladroit: clumsy.

    malapropos: inappropriate.

  Both words are normally applied to people's behaviour. The final syllable of *malapropos* rhymes with *low*.

malign, malignant, malevolent, malicious All mean *showing desire to injure* but with slightly different emphases.

    malign: having evil effects or influences. (Normally applied to things rather than people.)

    malignant: evil or highly injurious in its nature.

    malevolent: wishing ill; ill-disposed.

    malicious: motivated by mischief or viciousness; designed to cause harm (*malicious intent*).

  Only *malign* can be used as a verb: it means *defame*. Only *malignant* can be used of a disease, in which case it means *uncontrollable*.

Malevolent can be used only of people, whereas *malicious* and the stronger *malignant* can be used of things as well (*malicious gossip*, *malignant spread of unemployment*).

mandatory, statutory   Anything that is *mandatory* is compulsory because of an official instruction or command, but if it is *statutory* it is compulsory because of legislation. Parents have a statutory responsibility to have their children educated; it may be mandatory for the children to wear uniform to school.

Both words are stressed on the first syllable.

maniac, manic, maniacal   Technically, a *maniac* is a person suffering from a wild mental disorder, but more popularly he is a sane person whose behaviour is wild and disorderly or who has an excessive enthusiasm. *Manic* is the associated adjective, also found in *manic-depressive* (alternating between extremes of excitement and depression in a mentally disordered way). *Maniacal* (pronounced *man-EYE-ical*) too is adjectival, meaning *characteristic of a maniac or mania*.

mantle, mantel   *Mantel* exists only as the shelf over a fireplace or as the ornamental structure around it. *Mantle* has several meanings as a form of covering (especially of snow, fog or smoke) and is most frequently encountered in figurative use denoting a cloak symbolising status and authority.

marshal, martial   Although pronounced alike, these have nothing in common in their meanings. A *marshal* is either an officer of one sort or another, or a person who organises the arrangements for a parade. As a verb *marshal* means *assemble* or *arrange*. *Martial* is an adjective meaning *having to do with war or the military life*.

masochism: see **sadism**.

masterful, masterly

> *masterful*: determined to be master, dominating as a master; strong-willed, assertive, commanding.
> *masterly*: displaying the skill of a master of one's craft.

The corresponding nouns are *masterfulness* and *masterliness* but *mastery* does duty for both and is more common.

Masterful has the adverbial form *masterfully*. *Masterly* has no adverb, and one must resort to *in a masterly way/fashion*, etc.

maudlin, mawkish, sentimental   *Sentimental* may be used neutrally to describe something or somebody characterised by tender emotion

maunder, meander

or feeling rather than thought (*article of sentimental value; pay a visit for sentimental reasons*) but the word is also associated, disparagingly, with excessive, self-conscious or superficial emotionalism. Both *maudlin* and *mawkish* share this latter sense and bring something additional to it. *Maudlin* signifies tearfulness, *mawkish* a quality that is sickly, insipid, feeble, cloying or even nauseating.

See **sentiment**.

maunder, meander   To *maunder* is to talk (or, less commonly, to act or move) in a confused or aimless way. To *meander* is to wander aimlessly or on a winding course: it may be used of a thing, such as a path or river, or a person on the move, or of a person's thought-processes or speech.

mawkish: see **maudlin**.

maxim, axiom   An *axiom* is a self-evident or generally recognised truth, an established principle. A *maxim* is its succinct expression, especially as a rule of conduct.

maximise, increase   To *maximise* something is to *increase* it to a maximum, to make it as great or high as possible. To use *maximise* to mean no more than *increase* is wrong.

maximum: see **optimum**.

maybe, may be   *Maybe* means *perhaps* (*Maybe he'll come tomorrow*). When *may* is a verb, preceded by a subject and followed by *be*, the words must be written separately (*It may be that he'll come tomorrow*).

meantime, meanwhile, mean time

meantime (noun):	the intervening time, Mainly used in the phrase *in/for the meantime* though *in/for the meanwhile* is acceptable, if less common.
meanwhile (adverb):	during the intervening time; during the same time but somewhere else (*Meanwhile, it had started to snow*). The use of *meantime* in this way is common in informal speech, but should not be found elsewhere.

Mean time is found only in a few technical expressions such as *Greenwich mean time*.

mediums, media   Alternative plurals of *medium* (a means of communication, or a middle state between extremes – *a happy medium*).

Media is now invariable in the sense of *mass media* such as television or newspapers. It is quite clearly a plural, requiring the *media are/have*, etc., not *is/has*, though widespread ignorance of this fact may in the course of time require resigned acceptance of its use as a singular (*Television is a powerful media*). But not yet.

Medium is the normal plural for people acting as a channel of communication, such as those claiming to be an agency between the living and the dead.

melodic, melodious   *Melodious* means *tuneful. Melodic* may be used in this sense, but it is more commonly found as a technical word meaning *relating to melody* (as distinct from other musical elements such as rhythm or harmony): the *melodic line* (i.e. the tune) *in an orchestral piece may pass from one instrument to another.*

melted, molten   *Molten* (melted by heat) is applied only to metals. *Melted* (liquefied) is applied to other substances such as butter or chocolate.

memoranda, memorandums   The plural of *memorandum* may be either of these. The older, Latin plural *memoranda* is probably still more common than the more English form *memorandums*, but both may be ousted by the abbreviated *memos*, now recognised by dictionaries as standard (as is the singular *memo*). But *memorandas*, a sort of double plural, is illiterate.

mentality, mind   A person's *mind* is (roughly stated, for the word has many meanings) his ability to think; his *mentality* is the state or quality of his mind or his way of thinking. *Mentality* is often used to imply a warped or incomprehensible attitude of mind.

messenger: see **harbinger**.

meter, metre   *Metre* is the unit of length or a pattern of rhythm in poetry. *Meter* is needed in all other senses as a device for measuring a quantity (*parking/electricity meter*, etc.) or as a verb meaning *measure a flow.*

mettle, metal   *Metal* is familar enough and is therefore sometimes used when *mettle* is required. The latter means *strength of character or spirit, courage, stamina* and is found in such phrases as *on one's mettle* (aroused to make one's best efforts), *test one's mettle*, etc.

119

migrate, emigrate

>   *migrate*:   move from one locality (or country) to another (*migrated from the town to the country*).
>
>   *emigrate*:   leave one's country to live elsewhere.

To *migrate* may involve leaving one's country, but *emigrate* is the usual word for that. Another difference is that *migrate* implies being on the move (as *migrant* workers move in search of work) whereas *emigrate* implies a more official once-and-for-all move. *Migrate* is used too of animals or birds moving regularly to another region or climate for food or breeding grounds.

militate: see **mitigate**.

millipede: see **centipede**.

mind: see **mentality**.

minimal, small   *Minimal* is generally used as a showy, emphatic or vogue word meaning *small*. In fact it means *the smallest or least possible*.

minimise, reduce

>   *minimise*:   reduce to or estimate at the least possible amount or degree.
>
>   *reduce*:   make smaller or less.

The first is obviously more specific and extreme, and should never be used, as it commonly is, to mean merely the same as the second.

minister, administer   As a verb meaning *give aid*, *minister* is invariably followed by *to* (*ministered to their needs*). *Administer* is not. It means *manage* or *give out* and usually takes an object: *administer first aid/a drug/punishment*, etc.

misanthropist, misogynist   The first, more usually called a *misanthrope*, hates people in general; the second hates women.

mistrust: see **distrust**.

misuse, abuse   As verbs:

>   *misuse*:   use for a wrong purpose or in a wrong way.
>
>   *abuse*:   use badly; maltreat; speak insultingly.

In some contexts the words are interchangeable, but the main distinction is between doing something wrongly and doing it badly or viciously.

mite, might   The familiarity of *might* should not tempt one to

120

substitute it for the unfamiliar *mite* (a very small insect, child, coin or sum of money). *Mite* also occurs, informally, with the meaning *a little*. *He was a mite displeased* is the opposite of *He was mightily displeased*.

mitigate, militate   A very commonly confused pair.

> *mitigate*: moderate; lessen in severity, violence or evil. *Mitigating circumstances* are those that serve to lessen the seriousness of an offence.
>
> *militate*: have weight; tell (against); have influence or effect.

The usual error is to use the expression *mitigate against* which is nonsense and always wrong: *The scandal has not mitigated against him*; *Team changes have mitigated against a settled performance*. What is needed is *militate against*.

moat: see **mote**.

mobile, movable   Both mean *capable of being moved* but it is usually *movable* that is used in this sense and *mobile* in its additional sense of *capable of moving*. Hence a *movable cupboard* (as distinct from a built-in one) but *mobile home/warfare/crane* or a person who is *upwardly mobile* socially.

modern: see **contemporary**.

molten: see **melted**.

moment, momentum   *Moment* has several meanings, but the one that may give rise to confusion with *momentum* is *significance, importance*, as in *matters of moment*. The adjective is **momentous** (see next entry). *Momentum* is impetus gained from motion. A political movement, for example, may gather *momentum* and become something of *moment*, but that is to say two different things, not the same thing in two different ways.

momentary, momentous   *Moment* has two meanings, among others: *a very short period of time* and *importance, prominence* (as in *a matter of great moment*). *Momentary* relates to the first, *momentous* to the second. A *momentary lapse* is a brief one; a *momentous discovery* is a significant one.

momentum: see **moment**.

monogram, monograph

> *monogram*: design consisting of a letter or letters, often inter-woven initials, used as a decorative device.

monograph: treatise on a single, often restricted, area of scholarship.

monologue: see **dialogue**.

mooch, mope   Both mean *act in an aimless way* but *mooch* (which is informal) implies loitering or skulking whereas *mope* suggests gloomy or apathetic behaviour.

moot, mute   As an adjective, *moot* (rhyming with *boot*) is seldom encountered except in *a moot point*, an arguable matter. As a verb it means *bring up for discussion*. There is no relationship with *mute* (rhyming with *cute*) which means *silent, unspoken, dumb*, but a *mute point* and *the idea was muted* (instead of *moot* and *mooted*) are sometimes heard.

mope: see **mooch**.

moral, ethical, morale   *Moral* standards are those that relate to principles of what is right and wrong (especially, but by no means exclusively, in sexual matters). More loosely, a *moral* person is of good morals, i.e. virtuous. *Moral support* is support in matters of principle rather than in practical terms. *A moral victory* is a success of good over bad, even though it may be a defeat in practical terms. *A moral obligation* is a duty to do what is held to be right, as distinct from what is expedient or governed by self-interest, for example.

Ethical conduct is that which is governed by the moral principles agreed within a group or profession, e.g. the code of conduct which prevents doctors from soliciting a colleague's patients.

Morale (noun) is sense of confidence, pride, good spirits, feeling valued, or faith in what one is about.

See **ethic** and **amoral**.

morals: see **ethic**.

Moslem, Muslim, Islamic   *Moslem* and *Muslim* are variant spellings of the noun for an adherent of the religion of Islam. *Muslim* is now becoming the more usual of the two, a preference having been expressed by some Muslims themselves.

Both words are also adjectives (*a Muslim temple*) but *Islamic* should be used with abstractions (*the Islamic culture*).

mote, moat   A castle may have both.
mote: mound.

moat: trench, usually filled with water, protecting the perimeter. A *mote* is also a speck, usually of dust, but the word is rarely found.

motif, motive   *Motif* is the word for a central theme, dominating idea or repeated element in a work of art, though *motive* is sometimes used as a variant spelling in musical composition. Generally, however, *motive* is reserved for whatever causes someone to act.

Motif is pronounced *moat-eef*, with the stress on the second syllable.

movable: see **mobile**.

mowed, mown   Equally common and correct as alternative verb forms of *mow*, but adjectivally only *mown* may be used in front of a noun (*new-mown hay*).

multifarious, multitudinous

multifarious: having many parts; diverse.

multitudinous: very numerous.

The first implies an entity with many components (*company with multifarious business interests*; *financier with multifarious connexions*). The second (a rarer word, normally applied to people) merely implies great number.

munificent: see **magnanimous**.

munitions: see **ammunition**.

Muslim: see **Moslem**.

mute: see **moot**.

mutual, common, reciprocal   Purists argue that *mutual* means *experienced or expressed by two people about each other*, and that it is therefore wrong, or at least questionable, to speak of *our mutual enemy/friend* because that implies a relationship of at least three people (you, me and the enemy/friend). Likewise one should not refer to three or more people making an agreement *to their mutual benefit*. The correct word, it is argued, is *common* when more than two are involved, as in *common ground* or *common market*.

Mutual in reference to more than two is now unlikely to be ousted, but it is worth objecting to its frequently tautological use: it adds nothing to *mutual exchange of views*, *mutual cooperation/rivalry* or *come to a mutual understanding*.

Reciprocal can be used in place of *mutual* when it means *given by each of two to the other*, as in *reciprocal understanding*. Its more general sense is *given or done in return* (*He expects a reciprocal favour from me*) and *mutually corresponding*: a *reciprocal agreement* brings equivalent benefits to both sides, and *reciprocal action* is an equal response to an action taken by someone else. But this last example demonstrates a difference between *mutual* and *reciprocal*. *Mutual action* is taken by two people in concert; *reciprocal action* may be the same (as when an ally attacks and another ally takes *reciprocal*, i.e. similar, *action*) or it may be different, as when one side attacks and the other side takes *reciprocal*, i.e. equivalent, *action* against it.

mystical, mysterious
> *mystical*: relating to mysticism, the occult or the metaphysical.
> *mysterious*: puzzling, curious.

N

naive: see **ingenious**.

nationalise, naturalise Nowadays, *nationalise* is not much heard: *to put* (an industry, service, etc.) *under state control* is a notion that has lost political favour, and the different sound (but identical meaning) of *bring into public ownership* has now replaced *nationalise*, just as *denationalise* has given way to the less negative, more winning *privatise*.

To *naturalise* is to give citizenship to someone of foreign birth, though one can speak of a plant, animal or word becoming naturalised (i.e. adopted) in another region, country or environment: *café* is an example of a French word now fully *naturalised* in English.

naturalist, naturist
> *naturalist*: expert in or student of botany or zoology.
> *naturist*: nudist.

In writings about painting, a *naturalist* is someone who paints realistically (as compared with, say, a surrealist or an impressionist).

naught, nought Apart from its appearance in a few set expressions such as *come to/set at naught*, *naught* (meaning *nothing*) is archaic or literary. *Nought* is another word for the symbol *zero* (*to multiply by ten, add a nought*).

nauseating, nauseous These have the same meanings, a literal one of *causing nausea* (i.e. an inclination to vomit: *a nauseating smell*) and a figurative one of *disgusting, loathsome* (*a nauseous person*). In American English, however, *nauseous* may have the opposite meaning when applied to physical symptoms: it commonly means *feeling nausea*, not causing it. As is often the case, this American usage is increasingly seen and heard in British English. If *The cat is nauseous* can now have two opposite meanings, it is probably best to avoid *nauseous* when referring to literal sickness. The most common figurative uses are comparatively safe, however.

naval, nautical
> *naval*:   having to do with a navy (*naval battle, naval power*).
> *nautical*: having to do with ships, sailors or navigation (*nautical distance, nautical chart*).

The meanings overlap, and the adjective to use may be a matter of custom rather than of precise distinction. A *naval architect*, for example, is a person who designs ships, not necessarily for a navy, and a *nautical mile* is travelled by a navy as well as by a ship.

nefarious, felonious   *Felonious* is the more limited and technical word: it means *involving a serious crime*. *Nefarious* is a more general word meaning *evil, sinful, wicked*: *nefarious practices* may be underhand, immoral or dishonest without being criminal.

negligent, negligible, neglectful   The difference between *neglect* and *negligence*, such as it is, is that neglect is an action showing lack of duty and attention (*child died through neglect*) and negligence is a habit (or action) showing failure to exercise the carefulness expected of a prudent person (*accident caused by negligence*). Neglect is often deliberate, and negligence involuntary. The corresponding adjectives overlap, but if one is *neglectful* one is careless and forgetful (perhaps wilfully), especially in one's duty. If one is *negligent* one is culpably (often habitually) careless or simply unconcerned: the result is often a physical accident.

> *Negligible* means *insignificant*.

niceness, nicety   Both mean *the quality of being nice* but in practice their uses are distinct.
> *niceness*: pleasantness.
> *nicety*:   precision or subtlety of detail or quality (*to a nicety*, with exactness).

Niceties are refined formalities.

noisy, noisome   Unlike *noisy*, *noisome* has to do not with noise but

125

with annoyance: it means *disgusting* (especially in smell) or *harmful* (especially to health) or both (*a noisome drainage system*).

non-essential, inessential   Historically, *non-essential* is the opposite of *essential* in its usual meaning of *necessary*, and *inessential* is the opposite of *essential* meaning *inherent* as it does in *The essential quality of tragedy is. . . .* In common use the two are interchangeable, though careful writers prefer *non-essential* for *not necessary* and *inessential* for *extraneous*.

The two words may be used as nouns.

normality, normalcy   These have the same meaning, but the latter is American, ill-formed, unnecessary and avoidable.

north, northern   Custom dictates that we refer to *the North County* but *Northern England*, the *north wind* but the *northern hemisphere*, the *North Pole* but the *Northern Lights*. There is no discernible difference of meaning.

Capital letters are necessary as part of a formal title (*North Sea, North Star*) and advisable as a courtesy in *he comes from the North* or *North of England* or *is a Northerner*. See also the examples in the previous paragraph.

notable, noted, noticeable
> *notable*:   remarkable, prominent (usually applied to things, especially events: *a notable victory*).
> *noted*:   famous (usually applied to people: *a noted philosopher*).
> *noticeable*:   worthy of notice; perceptible.

A *notable change* is a considerable one; a *noticeable change* is simply one that can be noticed – it may be considerable or inconsiderable.

See **notorious**.

notorious, infamous   Both mean *well-known for some disreputable or wicked quality, deed or event*, but the emphasis in *notorious* is on the *well-known*, so much so that the word is sometimes – and ill-advisedly – used with no unfavourable connotation at all. The emphasis in *infamous* is on the *wickedness*, and the word may be used without much sense of *well-known*: a person's *infamous behaviour* is not necessarily generally known, though it usually is.

nought: see **naught**.

noxious, obnoxious   Something *noxious* is poisonous or harmful to health. The adjective is normally applied to physical substances, especially gas or fumes, though it is occasionally met in its figurative sense of *pernicious*. *Obnoxious* is a much more general word; meaning *extremely unpleasant*, it can be applied to people or things.

number: see **amount**.

numerous, innumerable
> *numerous*:   many, having many parts.
> *innumerable*:   countless.

For all practical purposes these are interchangeable (*We've been there on numerous/innumerable occasions*), except that *innumerable* is the more emphatic word.

nurture, cherish   These have *give care to* in common, but *cherish* has an emphasis on holding dear or keeping with affection whereas *nurture* implies nourishment, development and growth. *Cherish* has the additional meaning of *cling fondly* (to a hope or idea, for instance). *Nurture*, in keeping with its more active feel, also means *educate* or *train*.

O

object, objective   Both mean *an end towards which endeavours are directed*. *Objective* is best limited to *specific goal or target* (as it is in military terminology) and *object* to a more general sense of *purpose* (*the object of the exercise*; *the object of the policy is to. . . .*).

Only *object* can mean *person to whom action is directed* (*an object of pity*). It has several other meanings not confusable with *objective*.

Objective has become something of a vogue word, perhaps because of its military, no-nonsense feel, and is often used merely as an unnecessary lengthening of *object*.

oblige, obligate   *Obligate* is more common in American than in British English. It usually occurs in the form *obligated* (duty-bound) which has a tinge of the colloquial or even of dialect. Technically it means *constrain legally* (or *morally*) but in its everyday use it means nothing that is not contained in *oblige*.

oblivious: see **unaware**.

obnoxious: see **noxious**.

obscure, abstruse   *Difficult to understand*, but for different reasons: *obscure* because of unclear expression, *abstruse* because special knowledge is required.

    Obscure has several other meanings, of course.

observance, observation   An *observance* is an act of compliance with a law or custom, especially a religious practice. An *observation* is an act of watching or noticing, or a remark. To observe the speed-limit is *observance*, not *observation*.

obsolete, obsolescent
        obsolete: out of date; out of use.
        obsolescent: becoming *obsolete*.

obtrude, protrude
        protrude: stick out, project, thrust forwards.
        obtrude: thrust oneself (or something upon somebody) forward
                   in an unwelcome way.
    Protrude is normally used of a thing that projects, as a nail might stick out from a wall. *Obtrude* is used of people or things that impose themselves unduly, as a factory might obtrude on a rural landscope.
    See **obtrusive**.

obtrusive, intrusive   *Obtrusive* is mainly applied to something physical that is unwelcome by being too prominent (such as garish wallpaper), though it can be used of a person who pushes himself on one's attention or into one's privacy without permission or welcome. *Intrusive*, in contrast, is more commonly used of people, though it is sometimes applied to intangible things (*intrusive noise*).

    The main distinction is between *sticking out* and *pushing in*.

occidental: see **oriental**.

occupant, occupier   The person who owns a house is known formally as the *occupier*, informally as the *occupant*. Similarly, someone renting a flat, or using business premises, can be either the *occupant* (which has associations of temporary occupation) or the *occupier,* usually the former. But seats, beds, rooms, etc. can have only *occupants*.

occupied, preoccupied   Although the first is often used in place of the seond, there is a valuable distinction worth preserving.
        occupied: busy.
        preoccupied: engrossed (especially in one's own thoughts).

oculist, optician
> *oculist*:   specialist in eye-disorders or defects.
> *optician*:   person who sells (and sometimes makes) spectacles.

odious, odorous, odoriferous *Odorous* (having an odour or smell) is not as much used as its opposite *malodorous* (having an offensive odour). *Odoriferous* can mean the same as *odorous*, but it usually means *having a fragrant odour*. *Odious* means *hateful*, and has nothing to do with odour.

official, officious An *official* person or thing has formal authority (*official permission*); an *official dinner* has to do with people holding an office and is characterised by ceremony.
    An *officious* person is intrusive and meddlesome, offering unwanted advice or services, and often throwing his (usually petty) authority about.

older, oldest: see **elder**.

omnipotent, omniscient
> *omnipotent*: all-powerful.
> *omniscient*: all-knowing.

The difference is that between *potency* (power) and *science* (knowledge).

on to, onto Long resistance to the recognition of *onto* as a single word has now given way to acceptance of it, albeit rather grudgingly in some quarters. *On to* must be used when *on* is an adverb relating to a previous verb and *to* is either part of an infinitive (*He went on to become manager*) or a preposition with a meaning district from that of the *on* (*He went on to the top of his profession*), i.e. when the *on* expresses continuation and the *to* expresses direction. But when a single action is to be expressed (*Put it onto the back seat*) there can now be no objection, except insofar as *on* alone frequently suffices. It does not always do so, however: there is difference between *He reversed the car onto the road* and *He reversed the car on the road*.
    See **into, in to**.

onward, onwards There is no difference between these two as adverbs (*army moved onwards(s)*) or between them and *on*. Only *onward* is an adjective (*their onward progress*), often a tautological one.

operator, operative As well as being a person who runs a business, or a skilful manipulator of people or affairs (*a shrewd operator*), an *operator*

opposite, apposite

is someone who operates a machine (*telephone operator*), often one requiring skill. An *operative* is a less skilled person such as a manual labourer or factory worker: he may operate a machine, though a less complicated one.

opposite, apposite   *Apposite* means *apt*, (*highly*) *appropriate*, and is usually applied to something said or done (not to people). It has nothing to do with *opposite*.

optician: see **oculist**.

optimum, maximum, optimal   Whereas a *maximum* benefit/speed/ amount is the highest possible, an *optimum* or *optimal* one (the words mean the same) is the most advantageous or favourable, having regard to all the circumstances. A car's *maximum* speed may be 100 mph; its *optimum* speed, taking into account comfort, safety and fuel consumption as well as speed, and balancing all these factors, will almost certainly be lower.

Maximum and *optimum* are also nouns with these senses.

oral: see **aural**.

ordinal, cardinal   *Ordinal* numbers define something's position in a series (e.g. *second, fortieth*).

Cardinal numbers are those we count with (e.g. 2, 40).

ordinance, ordnance

    ordinance: decree; (religious) rite.

    ordnance: military supplies, notably artillery.

The latter word is normally found only in *ordnance survey* maps, originally drawn up under military auspices.

ordnance: see **ordinance**.

orgasmic, orgiastic   As colloquial terms of high praise, roughly meaning *wildly exciting*, these are interchangeable. More correctly, *orgasmic* is the adjective from *orgasm* (sexual climax) and *orgiastic* that from *orgy* (a gathering for sexual activity, drinking and immoderate indulgence generally).

Both *orgasm* and *orgy* can be used less literally, the first in the sense of *intense excitement*, the second in that of *frantic and excessive activity*, as in *an orgy of looting*, and so can their adjectives.

oriental, occidental

> *oriental*: of the East (normally considered to be east of the Mediterranean, especially East Asia).
>
> *occidental*: of the West (normally considered to be Europe and the USA).

The second word is not much used. The first is particularly applied to China and Japan.

oriented, orientated As they mean the same, the shorter version is preferable though probably less common. The excessive use of both words is turning them into jargon, sometimes tautological: a shop that is *customer-orientated* could hardly be anything else, one would think, though the expression is probably a fancy attempt to indicate that the shop-assistants are encouraged to be helpful. Both words deserve a rest: plain English alternatives such as *directed towards* are available.

ornate, ornamental

> *ornate*: elaborately decorated or adorned.
>
> *ornamental*: decorative, serving as an ornament.

An *ornamental* wall in a garden serves as an architectural decoration with no practical function: it may or may not be *ornate*.

orotund, rotund Applied to speech (especially to style of public speaking) or, less commonly, to choice of vocabulary and literary style, both can mean *pompous, bombastic, pretentious*. *Orotund*, confusingly, can also mean *dignified*, and *rotund* can mean *sonorous*. A feeling of roundness is common to both, and *rotund* can be used of people to mean *plump*.

It is in this sense that it is normally encountered, *orotund* being usually reserved to characterise speech or writing which is oratorical in style – consciously grand but rather inflated in manner and sense – though *rotund* occurs with this meaning.

ostentatiously, ostensibly

> *ostentatiously*: displaying pretentiously or to attract notice (*person who dresses ostentatiously*). Often used of display of wealth.
>
> *ostensibly*: apparently but not in reality; in a way intended for the sake of outward appearance and to conceal the truth (*burglar dressed ostensibly as a gas-board official*).

Both words imply disapproval, the first of vulgarity, the second of intention to deceive.

outdoor, outdoors   *Outdoor* is the adjective (*outdoor pursuits*), *outdoors* the adverb (*day when it is best to be outdoors*).

outward, outwards   *Outward* is adjective (*outward appearances*) and adverb (*outward bound*). *Outwards* is an alternative adverb only: it is chiefly used of physical movement (*search-party fanned outwards*).

overlook, oversee

overlook: fail to observe; disregard, excuse; have or give a view of from above, be higher than (*house overlooks the valley*).

oversee: supervise.

overtone, undertone   Apart from being a technical term in music, an *overtone* is an implication, usually in an individual word – an additional meaning or quality, sometimes a nuance, that the word suggests on top of its basic sense. There are examples in this dictionary of words with the same literal meaning but different overtones.

An *undertone* is a subdued sound (*speak in an undertone*) or colour, or an undercurrent of emotion or an underlying suggestion in something done or said – a sense of unarticulated feeling.

owing to: see **due to**.

P

pallet, palette

pallet: shaping-tool used by potter; straw mattress or bed; portable platform on which goods, especially containers, are stored and which can be moved (e.g. by fork-lift truck).

palette: board on which artists mix paints; range of colour characteristic of an artist or school of painting.

pandemic: see **epidemic**.

paranoiac, paranoid   The mental disorder characterised by delusions, usually of grandeur or persecution, is *paranoia*, and its two adjectives *paranoiac* and *paranoid* are interchangeable. Their debased use as substitutes for merely *suspicious, fearful without foundation*, or even *touchy*, is inexact, informal and unnecessary.

paraphrase: see **summary**.

parochial, provincial *Parochial* means *limited in interest*. *Provincial* may simply define fact: *provincial theatres* are those in the provinces, i.e. outside London. But if it is used, as it sometimes is, to mean *unsophisticated*, as in *provincial attitudes/taste*, etc., it carries a note of metropolitan snobbishness.

parricide, patricide

     parricide: murder of one's parent or close relative; person who does this.

     patricide: murder of one's father; person who does this.

  Parricide is sometimes used more broadly to mean the killing of one's fellow-countrymen in civil war.

part: see **portion**.

partake, participate Both mean *take a part or share*. *Participate* is chiefly used of joining actively with other people. *Partake*, a rarer word, is usually limited to taking a share of something, often food or drink.

partially, partly

     partly: in part(s).

     partially: not completely.

  If a rumour is *partly true*, it is true in parts and not in others. If an effort is *partially successful* it succeeds to a certain extent. A chair may be made *partly of wood* (not wholly); a person may be *partially deaf* (not fully). These distinctions are fine, and there are occasions when they are immaterial. A useful rule of thumb, however, is that *partly* is used of a part in relation to an identifiable whole, and *partially* of the extent of a quality.

participate: see **partake**.

particular, peculiar Among the meanings of *peculiar* is *distinct from others, exclusive,* as in a *belief peculiar to Buddhism*. In contrast, *particular* means *specific*. The two words overlap in their more general sense of *special, unusual* (*A particular/peculiar difficulty is that . . .*) though *particular* is the more common.

partly: see **partially**.

passed, past *Passed* is the past tense (*he passed*) and past participle (*Has

133

pathos

he passed?) of the verb *pass*. *Past* is noun (*the past*), adjective (*the past three days*), adverb (*walked past*) and preposition (*walked past me*; *past three o'clock*; *I would not put it past him*). Note the difference between *He has passed his driving-test* and *He is past his best*.

pathos: see **bathos**.

patricide: see **parricide**.

peaceable, peaceful

    peaceable: disposed to peace. (Usually applied to people and their behaviour.)

    peaceful: characterised by peace. (Usually applied to activity, atmosphere and times.)

  A person of *peaceable disposition* may not necessarily enjoy a *peaceful life*.

peculiar: see **particular**.

pedal, peddle(r), pedlar   A *pedal* is operated by the foot; to *pedal* is to operate a pedal. To *peddle* is to go about selling things (*peddle one's wares*) or promoting (e.g. scandal, gossip, ideas) persistently. A *pedlar* is one who peddles, but the more logical American spelling *peddler* is now commonly used of a person who peddles narcotics.

pendent, pendant

    pendent (adj.):   suspended; overhanging.

    pendant (noun):   suspended ornament, especially necklace with pieces of jewellery hanging from it.

  The spellings are interchangeable, but the ones given are the usual ones. *Pendent* is a little-used word.

pending, impending   Both can mean simply *imminent* but, depending on the context, *impending* can carry, additionally, a sense of threat or menace. *Pending* is more usually employed in its sense of *not yet decided or completed*.

peninsula, peninsular   The often misspelt noun is *peninsula*, and *peninsular* exists only as an infrequently required adjective.

perceptible, perceptive, percipient

    perceptible: able to be perceived; noticeable.

    perceptive: showing (quick or keen) perception; observant, discerning; having or showing sympathetic understanding.

Percipient means the same as *perceptive*. *Perceptible* does not mean *significant*.

See **perspicacious**.

peremptory, perfunctory
>   *peremptory*: urgent, commanding, imperious, decisive, dog-matic.
>   *perfunctory*: cursory, indifferent, done casually or superficially as a matter of routine.

Peremptory does not mean *sudden, abrupt* or *unthinking*, though a *peremptory summons/order/dismissal* may, of course, have some or all of such qualities

perennial: see **annual**.

perfervid: see **fervent**.

perfunctory: see **peremptory**.

perimeter, periphery, peripheral
>   *perimeter*: boundary round something flat.
>   *periphery*: external boundary or surface (especially of something round).

Perimeter is used of something precisely defined (*perimeter of an airfield*; *perimeter fence*). A *periphery* may be less precise (*the periphery of a town*) and its adjective *peripheral* is most commonly used to mean *of minor significance*: a *peripheral problem* is not a centrally important one.

periodic, periodical Interchangeable when meaning *intermittent* or *occasional* but *periodic* is the norm in technical contexts, notably scientific and mathematical ones (*periodic table/function/law*, etc.), and *periodical* in relation to publications appearing at regular intervals.

permanence, permanency
>   *permanence*: state of being permanent.
>   *permanency*: person or thing (e.g. job) that is permanent.

The second may be used (but seldom is) as an alternative to the first.

permeate, pervade Both mean *diffuse*, but *permeate* stresses penetration *through* or *into* something (*Marxism permeating universities*) whereas *pervade* stresses spread *throughout* every part of something (*smell pervading a kitchen*). Both are used literally and figuratively.

permissible, permissive
>   *permissible*:   allowable.

permissive: giving permission; tolerant, lenient.

Permissive has become a vogue word in such expressions as *the permissive society* and has now come to mean *indulgent* or *over-indulgent* in matters of social behaviour or sexual morality.

perpetrate, perpetuate

perpetrate: commit, be responsible for.

perpetuate: cause to continue or last indefinitely.

Perpetrate is used only of committing a crime, blunder or other outrage.

perquisite, prerequisite   A *perquisite* is an incidental profit, privilege or fringe benefit derived from one's employment or office. In this sense it is almost universally shortened to *perk*. The word also means anything claimed or held as an exclusive right. A *prerequisite* is something required beforehand – a pre-condition. The word also exists as an adjective meaning *required as a prior condition*.

See **requirement**.

persecute, prosecute   To *persecute* is to maltreat (someone), harass or pester, usually persistently, often for racial, religious or political reasons. To *prosecute* is to bring legal action (against someone) though it can also mean to carry out or follow through (a task, etc.)

persistent: see **consistent**.

personage, personality   *Personage* is rather an old-fashioned and formal word for someone of rank or distinction (or a person in fiction or history). *Personality* is a new-fangled usage denoting a celebrated or well-known person: its original meaning is *an individual's distinctive personal characteristics* as in *She has a lively personality*. *Personalities* are personal references of a kind thought to be irrelevant to a matter (*Don't bring personalities into the argument*).

personal, personnel   *Personnel* has been borrowed from the armed forces by commerce and industry as a pretentious, unnecessary but probably immovable substitute for *staff* (usually a large body of employees) and for the part of an organisation that deals with staff recruitment and welfare; hence *the personnel officer*. The spelling is un-English, as is the pronunciation (the stress is on the final syllable), and has to be distinguished from that of the familiar adjective *personal*.

personality: see **personage**.

136

personnel: see **personal**.

perspicacious, perspicuous
> *perspicacious*: having keen mental perception; acutely **perceptive**; discerning, shrewd.
> *perspicuous*: easily understood; lucid, clearly expressed.

The first is normally applied to people, the second to writing or speech.

For **perceptive** see **perceptible**. See also **perspicacity**.

perspicacity, perspicuity These are the nouns corresponding to **perspicacious, perspicuous**.

pertinacity: see **tenacity**.

perturb: see **disturb**.

peruse, scan, read *Peruse* and *scan* are strange words in that they have come to mean something almost opposite to their original sense. Properly they mean *read carefully*, but loosely they have come to mean merely *read* or even *read casually or quickly*. Until they settle down into some less ambiguous state they are best avoided in favour of *read*, with or without an adverb such as *attentively* or *rapidly*. *Scan* is unambiguous, however, in the sense of *pass a beam over a surface* (e.g. part of the body) *to examine it*.

pervade: see **permeate**.

perverse, perverted
> *perverse*: deliberately wrong-headed, stubborn, uncooperative, unreasonable.
> *perverted*: having abnormal, deviant or corrupt (moral) standards, beliefs or practices (especially in sexual conduct); morally deformed.

See **perversity**.

perversity, perversion These are the nouns corresponding to **perverse, perverted**.

phantom, phantasm, phantasmagoria The first two mean *ghost*, but a *phantasm* is also an illusion or figment of the imagination. A *phantasmagoria* is a dream-like, confused and shifting succession of real or imagined things or people.

For **phantasm** see also **fantasy**.

pharisaic, philistine   As adjectives,
    pharisaic: hypocritical, self-righteous.
    philistine: hostile or indifferent to (or lacking in) culture.
  The words derive from the biblical proper nouns *Pharisee* (a person obsessed with the rules rather than the spirit of religion) and *Philistine* (an enemy of the Israelites). Hence a *philistine* (small *p*) suffers from *philistinism* (hostility or indifference to culture) but *pharisaic* has no such relations in general use.

phase, phrase   As a noun, a *phase* is a period or stage in a sequence (*the early phase of the war*) or cycle (*phases of the moon*) though the word has several other technical meanings in science. As a verb it means *carry out gradually*, normally in planned stages (*troops in a phased withdrawal*).
  A *phrase* is a group of words; as a verb, the word means *express in words*.

phenomenon, phenomena   The latter is the plural of the former. It is sometimes used erroneously as a singular: *a phenomena* or *the phenomena is* are wrong.
  Some dictionaries admit the more English plural *phenomenons*, but it is rare, shows no signs of catching on, and would be regarded by many as illiterate.

philistine: see **pharisaic**.

phrase: see **phase**.

picaresque, picturesque   *Picaresque* is a literary term used to describe the type of story in which a rogue passes through a series of adventures. *Picturesque* means *pleasant* (especially *quaint*) when applied to a scene, and *vivid* when applied to language.

picket, piquet   *Piquet* is a card-game when pronounced with a stressed second syllable sounding like *ket* (or *kay*). It also survives (rhyming with *wicket*) in military jargon as a word for a small body of troops left on guard. A *picket* is, correspondingly, a person standing outside a place of work during a strike to dissuade employees from working; this spelling is a common alternative to the military *piquet* nowadays.

picturesque: see **picaresque**.

piebald: see **dappled**.

piquant, pungent   Both mean *sharp* but *piquant* has the sense of *agreeable* (*piquant wit*, for example) while *pungent* does not (*pungent* *criticism* is biting). Also *piquant* is used of taste, *pungent* more usually of smell.

Piquant is pronounced with the stress on the first syllable, which sounds like *pea*; the second syllable is pronounced *k'nt* (or *karnt*).

piquet: see **picket**.

piteous, pitiable, pitiful   All three can mean *arousing or deserving pity* and are interchangeable in this sense. *Pitiable* and *pitiful* also share the meaning of *arousing contempt* (because of inadequacy), though it is *pitiful* that is most frequently used in this way (*The government has offered a pitiful amount*). *Pitiable* is usually found in the sense of *deplorable*, applied to suffering (*child found in a pitiable condition*). *Piteous*, the least used of the three, normally means *exciting compassion*, as in *the injured's piteous moans*.

plain, plane   Both words have several meanings, *plain* chiefly as an adjective (and as a noun meaning a *level stretch of country*), *plane* chiefly as a noun (and as an adjective meaning *level* or *flat* as in *a plane surface*). It is these parenthetical definitions that may give rise to confusion.

The main uses of *plane* (apart from mathematical ones) are as a noun for *smoothing-tool* and *level of consciousness* (*on the moral/intellectual plane*), an abbreviation for aeroplane, and a verb meaning *skim* and *smooth with a plane*. *Plain* is never a verb, and exists as a noun only in the one sense quoted above.

plaintive, plaintiff   *Plaintiff* is legal only: it denotes the person who brings a civil action in a court. *Plaintive* is the adjective for *expressing sadness*.

plane: see **plain**.

pleasantry, pleasantness   A *pleasantry* is an agreeable remark, usually made in the interests of politeness or a joke. *Pleasantness* is the state of being pleasant or giving pleasure.

poetic, poetical   *Poetic justice*, *poetic licence* and *poetic drama* are invariable. One would also be inclined to speak of someone's *poetical works/writings* as distinct from his plays or short stories. That apart, the two words are interchangeable, *poetic* being the more common.

politic, political   When applied to a person, *politic* means *prudent* (especially in manipulative dealings with other people). When applied to a thing, it means *expedient*. *Political* relates to government policy-making and (party) politics.

populace, populous   These are pronounced alike, and have to do with people, but
> *populace* (noun):   the local inhabitants; the people (slightly derogatory).
> *populous* (adjective): having many inhabitants.

pore, pour   Usually followed by *over*, *pore* means *study closely* or *think deeply* (*about*), and has nothing to do with rain, tea, oil or cold water.

portion, proportion, part
> *portion*:   a share of a whole.
> *proportion*: a part in relation to a whole.
> *part*:   a constituent of a whole.

One speaks of a *part* of a city but a *portion* of a pie. The *proportion* of boys in a mixed school is the number of boys reckoned in relation to the total number of pupils.

All three words have other, less related meanings.

See also **proportional**

pose, propose   The meanings of both include *put forward*, but *pose* is used of a question for consideration or response and *propose* of a plan for consideration or adoption.

potent, potential
> *potent*:   powerful, effective.
> *potential*: possible but not yet (made) actual.

pour: see **pore**.

practical, practicable
> *practical*:   useful in practice.
> *practicable*: capable of being put into practice.

Applied to a person, *practical* means *good at doing things*.

Something that can be brought about is *practicable*, but only that which is useful, beneficial, successful, etc. is *practical*. *The plan is not practicable* means that it cannot be put into effect. *The plan is not practical* means that it can be put into effect but will not succeed. A plan, therefore, may be *practicable* without being *practical*, but it cannot be *practical* without being also *practicable*.

See **pragmatic**.

practice, practise *Practice* is the noun (*makes a practice of exercising regularly*), *practise* the verb (*does not practise what he preaches*). It helps to remember *advice* (noun) and *advise* (verb) where the pronounciation is a guide to the correct spelling.

pragmatic, practical *Pragmatic* is a vogue word used as if it meant the same as *practical*. It does not. A *practical* person is one not given to theory, who is good at doing things or getting them done. A *pragmatic* person has an attitude of mind that is concerned with practical consequences or expediency rather than with theory or dogma. Pragmatism is a way of thinking about things, not necessarily of doing them.

See **practical**.

pray, prey Few people seem to have difficulty with *prey* in the sense of a hunted animal or human victim (*became a prey to anxiety*) or in the related verbal sense of *hunt* or *make a victim of*, but the more abstract verbal sense *affect distressingly* (as in *the problem preyed on his mind*) sometimes invites confusion with *pray* (address prayers).

precede, proceed
>   *precede*:   go or be before (in time, place, order, importance, etc.); introduce, preface.
>   *proceed*:   go ahead (usually after a pause); advance; originate (*The complaint proceeds from a misunderstanding*).

Precede has the emphasis of *being in front of*. *Proceed* has that of *going forward*.

See **procedure**.

preceding, precedent, precedence *Preceding* is the adjective related to **precede**; it means *being or going before*. *Precedent* can mean the same, but it is almost always found as a noun meaning something (e.g. a decision, happening or example) used to justify something similar that takes place in the future; in such contexts as *the storm was without precedent* it means *something similar that happened in the past*. *Precedence* is the act or state of *preceding* (i.e. being or going before), the right to preferential treatment, the order that governs preferential treatment, or priority in status.

See **precede**.

precipitate, precipitous These are frequently confused.
>   *precipitate*:   rash; violently hurried (*a precipitate decision*).

141

precipitous: like a precipice, extremely steep (*half-way up a precipitous slope*).

The common error, notably among politicians, is to use *precipitous* when *precipitate* (over-hasty) is needed.

précis: see **resumé**.

predestined: see **destined**.

predetermined: see **destined**.

predict, predicate To *predict* is to foretell. *Predicate* is a rare verb which means, apart from its special sense in logic, *affirm* or *imply*, though it is being increasingly and spuriously used in its American sense of *base* as in *The policy is predicated on. . .*

predominate, preponderate These share the senses of *prevail, be the chief element, hold the advantage in number or quantity. Predominate* is the more popular of the two (*Men still predominate in the legal profession*). *Preponderate* has the special sense of *weigh more, be heavier* and is thus the better word to signify greater power, force or influence. *Predominate* means more generally *have control* or *be superior*.

See **dominate**.

pre-empt, prevent To *pre-empt* is to take or do something before anyone else can, thus frustrating somebody or something: it also means *to appropriate.* That is not the same as *prevent* (stop something from happening or being; stop someone from doing something) which lacks the sense of getting in first.

There is some doubt about the correctness of *pre-empt somebody* (rather than something): *forestall* is safe.

preface, prefix, prologue

preface: something introductory or preliminary, usually a statement at the front of a book explaining its scope and method.

prefix: addition, usually a syllable, to the beginning of a word (e.g. *un* + *familiar*) to produce a variation in meaning; title before a person's name (e.g. Mrs, Dr).

prologue: introduction, usually to a play, drawing attention to its theme; a preliminary act or event (*uprising was a prologue to a general war*)

Preface and *prefix* (but not *prologue*) are used as verbs. *Preface* is normally followed by *with* or *by* and means *introduce (by)* or *furnish (with) a preface. Prefix* is normally followed by *to* and means *add to the beginning of.* One may *preface* a speech *with* a few jokes or *prefix* a few jokes *to* a speech.

preliminary: see **preparatory**.

premature, previous These overlap on occasions. A decision may be described as *premature* if it is felt to be unduly early; more informally or jocularly it may be said to be 'a bit *previous*'. Apart from that, the words are clearly differentiated:
> *premature*: occurring before the expected or normal time; impulsive, hasty.
> *previous*: coming before something else.

premise, premiss Used as nouns, these are interchangeable (pronounced to rhyme with the first two syllables of *premises*) though *premise* is the more normal spelling. They mean a statement (or, in logic, one of the propositions in a syllogism) from which a conclusion is drawn, or a presupposition. Only *premises*, however, can be used of buildings.

   Premise is also a verb meaning *state or assume* (something) *as a premise or premiss* in an argument; *presuppose*.

premonition, presentiment A *premonition* is a warning, a *presentiment* a feeling, that something unpleasant is going to happen. When a *premonition* comes to one as an intuition, without conscious reason, it is indistinguishable from a *presentiment*. However, it can also be a warning coming from outside the self (*His resignation should have been a premonition that the firm was in difficulties*); *presentiment* cannot be used in this sense.

preoccupied: see **occupied**.

preparatory, preliminary Both are used in the sense of *introductory*, but more precisely *preparatory* means *preparing for what follows* whereas *preliminary* does not necessarily have the sense of preparation and merely means *coming before*, usually before something of a more important nature.

preponderate: see **predominate**.

prerequisite: see **requirement** and **perquisite**.

prescribe, proscribe
> *prescribe*: lay down as a rule or course to be followed.
> *proscribe*: forbid (by law); exile; reject as dangerous.

presentiment: see **premonition**.

preserve: see **conserve** and **reserve**.

pressurise, pressure, press *Pressurise* is an unnecessary word except in the scientific sense of *arrange to maintain normal or near-normal atmospheric pressure* as in an aircraft's pressurised passenger compartment. In the more familiar sense of *bring pressure to bear* (on someone in order to influence him) *pressure* is a better alternative, being shorter and simpler, as is *press* which can also mean the same.

presume: see **assume**.

presumptuous, presumptive
>*presumptuous*: bold, insolent, taking liberties, undertaking without leave, forward.
>*presumptive*: providing reasonable ground for belief.

Careless pronunciation of the first invites the misspelling *-ious*.

pretence, pretension, pretentiousness A real or implied claim to distinction, especially when unsupported, is *pretence* or *pretension* (which also means an effort to make such a claim). *Pretentiousness* is the making of such a claim. Other distinctions include:
>*pretence*: false show (or doing something), make-believe; professed intention (*false pretences*).
>*pretentiousness*: ostentatious display (especially by person pretending to be other than he is).

prevaricate, procrastinate Even though both imply degrees of disapproval, especially in the language of political abuse, there is no excuse for muddling two quite distinct words as often as people do.
>*prevaricate*: speak or act with intent to deceive.
>*procrastinate*: put off (something) until later.

Nor does *prevaricate* mean *hesitate*.

prevent: see **pre-empt**.

preventive, preventative *Preventative* is an unnecessary lengthening of *preventive*, which means the same and is to be preferred. It means *serving to prevent or hinder*: preventive medicine is intended to avert disease in advance rather than cure it after it occurs. *Preventive* is also a (rare) noun meaning *something that prevents*.

previous: see **premature**.

prey: see **pray**.

priceless: see **worthless**.

primary, prime   Both mean *first in importance* and *fundamental*; either the nouns they go with are determined by convention (*prime minister*) or the adjectives are interchangeable (*prime/primary reason, consideration, cause*, etc.). The general distinction is that *primary* is *first in time or position* (*primary election*) and *prime* is *first in value or quality* (*prime meat*). *Primary* also means elementary (*primary education*) and *first-hand*: solar power is a *primary* (i.e. direct) source of power but not yet a *prime* (important) one; electricity is a *prime* one but not a *primary* one, because it is manufactured, not first-hand.

primeval, primitive   Anything that belongs to the earliest ages of the world or is characteristic of them may be described by either adjective, but only *primitive* means *crude, elementary* or *old-fashioned*.

principal, principle   One of the hoariest favourites of grammar books. *Principal* is *chief* either as adjective (*the principal reason*) or noun (*college principal*). A *principle* is a fundamental truth, law of nature, code of right conduct, or moral formula (*will not do it on principle*); the word exists only as a noun.

prise, prize, pry

> *prise*:   force out or open, literally by levering (*prise open the lid*) or (figuratively) with difficulty (*prise the truth out of them*).
> *prize*:   value highly (*a prized possession*).
> *pry*:   peer or inquire closely, inquisitively or impertinently (*pry into other people's affairs*).

   Prise is often spelt with a -*z*, which must be regarded as acceptable, but it is sensible to insist on the -*s* spelling to distinguish it from an entirely different word.

   Prize is the only possible spelling for the sense quoted. The word is also a noun for an award or reward, and an adjective meaning *outstanding* (*a prize idiot*).

   Confusingly, *pry* is American for *prise* and is sometimes found on food packages (*Pry open*). This is indefensible.

   Pry has the forms *pries* (rhyming with *prise* and *prize*!) and *pried*.

privation: see **deprivation**.

prize: see **prise**.

problem: see **dilemma**.

procedure, proceedings

procedure: (established) way of acting or progressing (*follow the correct procedure in applying for a passport*).

proceedings: events, going-on; legal action; transactions or minutes (of a meeting).

To follow a *legal procedure* is to take the correct legal *steps* to accomplish something; *legal proceedings* are an *action* in court.

proceed: see **precede**.

proceedings: see **procedure**.

proclivity, propensity Although both signify *natural tendency or inclination*, there is an important distinction in that *proclivity* connotes inclination towards something disreputable. *Propensity* does not, and also suggests a slightly weaker degree of predisposition.

Proclivity is often found as a plural with a singular meaning (*sexual proclivities*).

procrastinate: see **prevaricate**.

procure, secure In the sense of *obtain* or *bring about* these are generally interchangeable, though *procure* (a slightly formal word) suggests acquisition by care or effort and *secure* has overtones of making sure or of acquisition for a certain purpose. *Procure* also means *obtain for prostitution*, and *secure* has a number of familiar senses that do not overlap with *procure*.

prodigy, progeny, protégé(e)

prodigy: person (especially child) with exceptional abilities or qualities; a marvellous thing.

progeny: offspring, descendants.

protégé: male person (often young) with an influential protector, patron or guide. Also *protégée*, a female person in this position.

proficiency, efficiency

proficiency: expertise in an art, skill, occupation or branch of learning.

efficiency: ability to produce good results with the least waste of effort.

It follows that only people have *proficiency*; both people and things can demonstrate *efficiency*.

See **efficacy**.

profligate, prolific
> *profligate*: wildly extravagant or wasteful; immoral.
> *prolific*: abundantly productive (*a prolific journalist*).

progeny: see **prodigy**.

prognosis: see **diagnosis**.

programme, program *Programme* is the English spelling, *program* the American. The latter spelling is now established in British English in computer language, but nowhere else.

prohibit: see **inhibit**.

prolific: see **profligate**.

prologue: see **preface**.

prone, supine
> *prone*: lying face downwards.
> *supine*: lying on one's back.

In practice *prone* is generally used of a person or animal lying flat or still, often on the ground, in whatever position, and *supine* is normally found in its figurative sense of *indolent, lethargic, passive, inactive*.

For another sense of **prone** see **likely**.

pronounce: see **announce**.

propensity: see **proclivity**.

prophecy, prophesy The *-sy* is pronounced as *sigh*, the *-cy* as the first syllable of cynic.

Prophecy is the noun, *prophesy* the verb. To *prophesy* is to make a *prophecy*.

propitious: see **auspicious**.

proportion: see **portion**.

proportional, proportionate Both mean *in proper proportion* (see **portion, proportion**), but *proportional* is normally used before a noun and *proportionate* after a noun or verb and before *to*. If an insurer pays out money in *proportional sums*, it is not shared haphazardly but in due proportion to something, e.g. the relative merits of the recipients' claims. In other words, people receive amounts *proportionate* to their loss.

The opposites are *disproportional* and *disproportionate*, but many people use the latter to do duty for the former. Both mean *out of*

147

proportion, unequal, and *disproportionate* carries the sense of *excessive*. A problem that takes up a *disproportionate* amount of time consumes an amount not equalling the value of the result or exceeding what is normally needed.

proposal, proposition To make (put forward, etc.) a *proposal* is to put forward a plan, offer, idea or suggestion for action. A *proposition* is something put forward for consideration. This distinction, always a very fine one, has become blurred by the recent widespread use of *proposition* to mean *a person or matter requiring (special) consideration* (*The exam is a tough proposition*) and as a verb meaning *propose sexual intercourse*. These usages are still new enough to be regarded as informal.

propose: see **pose**.

proposition: see **proposal**.

propound, expound
>   *propound*: put forward for consideration.
>   *expound*: explain (argument, etc.) in detail.

proscribe: see **prescribe**.

prosecute: see **persecute**.

prostate, prostrate

prostrate (verb):	lay (oneself) on ground in submission; reduce to submission or exhaustion. (Pronounced with the stress on the second syllable.)
prostrate (adjective):	lying full-length in submission or adoration; physically or emotionally weakened. (Pronounced with the stress on the first syllable.)

This word is occasionally confused but has nothing to do with the *prostate* (or *prostate gland*) in men.

protagonist: see **antagonist**.

protégé(e): see **prodigy**.

protrude: see **obtrude**.

proven, proved, unproven The first two are alternative past participles of *prove*. *Proved*, which rhymes with *moved*, is the more common

(*It has proved to be very popular*) though American English prefers
proven, which is also current in the *not proven* verdicts permitted by
Scottish law. As an adjective before a noun, *proven* – the first syllable
rhymes with *stove* – is normal (*a proven liar*).

Unproven rather than *unproved* is the usual negative, certainly as
adjective and probably as past participle, though *That is unproved* is not
incorrect.

provided, providing   As an expression of stipulation, *provided* is best
followed by *that* (*The race will go ahead provided that the sea remains
calm*). The omission of *that* is common and acceptable but a shade
informal. The alternative *providing* (with or without *that*) is equally
authentic but unnecessary.

provincial: see **parochial**.

provoke, evoke   These share the sense of *stimulate*, but the *pro-* means
forth, forward and *e-* means *from*, so *provoke* implies a putting forward
and *evoke* a drawing out. An action may *provoke* (anger) a person or
provoke (cause) an argument; it may *evoke* (attract) someone's pity or
evoke (call up) memories.

For **evoke** see also **evince**.

prudish, prurient
    prudish: having an extreme or excessive modesty, primness or
             propriety, especially regarding sexual matters.
    prurient: having or arousing an excessive and unhealthy interest
             in sexual matters.

pry: see **prise**.

psychiatrist, psychologist   The first deals with mental disease, the
second with the mind and its activity more generally. A *child
psychiatrist* is concerned with mental disorder in the young, an
educational psychologist with mental functions (e.g. the intelligence)
related to the education of the young.

A *psychiatrist* is a medical practitioner; a *psychologist* need not be.
See **psychic**.

psychic, psychiatric   The *psych-* form indicates reference to the mind
(*psychology, psychopath*, etc.). *Psychiatric*, pronounced with emphasis
on the *-a-*, is the adjective from *psychiatry*, the branch of medicine
concerned with mental disorder. Whatever is *psychic* lies outside the

sphere of the physical, and is related to the supernatural or occult. See **psychiatrist**.

psychologist: see **psychiatrist**.

puerile: see **juvenile**.

punctual, punctilious   Someone who is *punctilious* pays scrupulous attention to correctness in etiquette and conventions, or more particularly to duties and to detail. He will almost certainly be *punctual*, though a person who is *punctual* is not necessarily *punctilious* in other respects.

pungent: see **piquant**.

punish: see **sanction**.

purport, purpose   Anything or anybody who *purports* (i.e. claims) to be or do something is under suspicion of doing so falsely or unsuccessfully: *a book purporting to unravel the mystery of Jack the Ripper* has either failed or turned out to be something else, such as an attack on Victorian hypocrisy. The less common verb *purpose* (*have as an intention*) has no such colouring. The same distinction carries over somewhat into the nouns: a *purpose* is, neutrally, an intention whereas a *purport* is a professed or ostensible meaning, often (but not necessarily) with the implication that the real meaning is different.

purposely, purposefully
    purposely: on purpose, intentionally.
    purposefully: in a determined manner, resolutely.

Q

quantitative, qualitative   The difference is that between quantity and quality. To subject a proposal to *quantitative analysis* is to work out what quantities (e.g. of money) it would need; *qualitative analysis* is an examination of quality or merit.

Being something of a mouthful, *quantitative* is giving way to the acceptable variant *quantitive*, but there is no similar shorter form of *qualitative*.

quantity: see **amount**.

query, inquiry A *query* is a question. An *inquiry* may be the same – a request for information – or it may be a series of questions, i.e. an investigation.

One normally *raises* a *query*, *makes* an *inquiry* (in the sense of *request*) or *conducts* an *inquiry* (in the sense of *investigation*).

See **enquiry**.

question: see **interrogate**.

queue: see **clue**.

quiet, quietness, quietude All are nouns denoting freedom from disturbance. The distinction, such as it is, is that *quietness* and *quietude* are a habitual state of tranquillity and *quiet* an occasion of it (*I'd like some peace and quiet*). In practice, *quiet* and *quietness* are interchangeable except in some stock expressions: *on the quiet*, for example, is invariable, meaning *discreetly*. *Quietude*, the rarer word, is always used of a condition or state of tranquillity, often applied to landscape.

quirky: see **kinky**.

quit, quitted These are alternative past tense and past participle forms of the verb *quit* meaning *leave* or *resign*. The shorter form, long favoured in America, appears to be gaining ground, but there is still a slight preference for *quitted* as past particple.

In the sense of *stop*, *quit* (never *quitted*) is American and informal (*quit talking/smoking/moaning*, etc.).

quote, cite One may either *quote* or *cite* a person or thing as an illustration, precedent, authority or proof, but only *quote* a price or estimate or (usually) specific words which are being repeated. *Cite* also means *name by way of commendation*.

R

racist, racialist Like *racism* and *racialism*, *racist* and *racialist* cannot be differentiated between, except to say that the short form is the newer, more punchy and more common.

rack, wrack Nowadays *wrack* is likely to be encountered only in *wrack and ruin* (destruction, collapse) and even there the spelling *rack* is both

racket, racquet

acceptable and sensible. *Rack* is obligatory in all other senses as noun (*rack and pinion*) and verb (*rack one's brain*), though *wrack* may be found in specialist contexts as a (rare) word for seaweed, and in literature with meanings now obsolete.

racket, racquet A *racquet* is an implement used in tennis and some other games. *Racket* is an alternative spelling, and also the only spelling of the word in all its other senses (e.g. *uproar*, *fraudulent enterprise*, etc.). The two words are pronounced alike.

raise, raze Roughly speaking, *raise* has to do with upward movement and *raze* with the opposite because its most common meaning is *make level with the ground, destroy*, usually in *raze to the ground* by fire, explosion, etc.

See also **rise** and **rear**.

rapacious, voracious

    rapacious: excessively greedy, covetous or grasping; (of animal, especially bird) feeding on living prey.

    voracious: eating great quantities; insatiable (*voracious reader/appetite*, etc.).

rapt, wrapped *Rapt* is *enraptured* (*a rapt expression on their faces*) and *wholly absorbed* (*listen with rapt attention*). Among the senses of *wrap* is *engross, involve completely*, especially in the expression *wrapped up in* (one's family, work, etc.). One may therefore be *rapt in thought* or *wrapped in thought*: the punctilious will use the former to suggest a state of trance and the latter to imply mere abstraction (by analogy with *mountain wrapped in mist*). But few will recognise such subtlety.

rare, scarce Both are applied to what is found only occasionally or in small amounts, and they may sometimes be interchangeable (*That sort of service is a very rare/scarce commodity*).

Rare, however, has the emphasis *unusual* (and therefore often valuable) as in *rare painting/kindness/treat* whereas *scarce* means *insufficient to meet demand* as in *Strawberries are scarce this year*.

rational: see **reasonable**.

ravage, ravish

    ravage: damage badly (*countryside ravaged by a storm*).

    ravish: fill with delight (*ravishing beauty*); rape, violate.

See **ravished**.

ravished, ravenous   Probably as a result of confusion between *ravenous* (i.e. *very hungry*) and *famished*, *ravished* is sometimes used as if it meant the same. It does not: it means *delighted* or *raped* and should therefore be used with special care.

See **ravage**.

raze: see **raise**.

read: see **peruse**.

readable, legible   These share the sense *able to be deciphered* as in *handwriting that is not very readable/legible* but *legible* is the more common (certainly when applied to something hand-written). *Readable* is best reserved for a meaning that *legible* does not share — *easy and interesting to read*.

See **illegible**.

reap, wreak   These normally occur only in a limited number of stock expressions which include *reap the benefit* and *wreak one's revenge*. This may appear to imply that both words mean *enjoy* and are interchangeable. They are not, though they are sometimes confused. *Reap* means *gain as a reward or result* and *wreak* means *cause*, usually harmfully (*wreak havoc*).

rear, raise   Grammar books used to insist that one should *rear* children and *raise* (or *rear*) animals. The words are now interchangeable; if anything, it is more normal to *raise* a family and *rear* sheep.

See also **raise** and **rise**.

reasonable, rational   Whatever is *reasonable* is in accordance with common sense and avoids extremes: whatever is *rational* is in accordance with logic and man's capacity to reason. Behaviour which is not *reasonable* is not sensible; if it is not *rational* it is illogical or insane.

rebound, redound   To *rebound* is to bounce or spring back, as a ball may *rebound* from a wall. When abstract things such as plans or intentions *rebound*, the implication is usually that they damage their instigator.

To *redound* is to have an effect, usually an advantageous one: *If it succeeds it will redound to your credit* (though it is possible for things to *redound to* one's disadvantage).

Redound has another and less frequently used sense of *recoil* (upon, to) or *come back* as in *benefits that redound to mankind because of his self-sacrifice*. When the word is used in this way in contexts which have to do with adverse consequences it is synonymous with *rebound* (*His arrogance redounded on his own head when he was dismissed for exceeding his authority*). This sense is best avoided, as it may sound like ignorant confusion with *rebound*, and it is unnecessary anyway: the definitions given in the first two paragraphs are sufficient for most eventualities. See **resound**.

rebuff: see **rebut**.

rebuke, reproach

>   *rebuke:*   scold, reprimand.
>   *reproach*:   express disappointment (with person) for incorrect conduct.

The first is a stronger word than the second. Another difference is that one may *reproach* but not *rebuke* oneself, i.e. feel regret for one's own behaviour.

rebut, rebuff

>   *rebut*:   disprove (an argument by putting forward a contrary one).
>   *rebuff*:   snub; reject (usually sympathy, help); beat back or reject (an attack).

recall, recollect   Both mean *remember* but only *recall* means *order to return* and *revoke, take back, cancel*.

recant, retract   To *recant* is to withdraw or repudiate one's former belief or statement, especially a religious or political one, in a public or even formal way. *Retract* is a less grand and more general word: it means *take back, refuse to abide by, go back on* (for example a confession, promise or agreement) or *draw back* or *in* (as an aircraft *retracts* its undercarriage or a cat its claws).

reciprocal: see **mutual**.

reckless: see **feckless**.

recollect: see **recall**.

reconciliation, conciliation   *Conciliation* is appeasement or overcoming hostility; it is a word much used of satisfying both sides in an industrial dispute. *Reconciliation* is more than that. When applied to people it means restoration of former friendship or acquiescence in something unpleasant (*reconciliation with one's fate*). Applied to things it means the creation of compatibility (*reconciliation of differing points of view*).

re-count, recount   The hyphen is crucial:
> *re-count*: count again.
> *recount*: narrate.

recoup, recuperate   Misunderstanding arises not only because these sound as if they are related but also because they share the sense of *regain*.
> *recoup*:   make good (a loss, especially financial); compensate (someone) for (a loss).
> *recuperate*:   recover (e.g. money), regain one's former health.

The two overlap in the sense of making good a loss (but not in other ways), but *recover* is probably a better word than *recuperate* in this sense.

recourse, resource, resort   Much confusion is caused by these similar-sounding words, all of which have to do with turning to someone or something for help (though *resource* and *resort* have other meanings). The confusion is not so much in meaning as phraseology.

Recourse and *resort* are nouns meaning *a person or thing* (e.g. a course of action) *turned to for help*; additionally *resource* may be used in this way of a thing but not a person. *Resort* is often found in *As a/in the last resort*. Examples of the other two words in action are *Our only recourse* (i.e. course of action) *is to sell up* and *Cowardice is his usual resource* (i.e. source of aid). It would be possible to substitute *resort* in both of these.

Recourse and *resort* (but not *resource*) can also mean *the act of turning* (to person or thing) *for help*. The usual forms are *to have recourse to* or (infrequently) *have resort to*, which mean the same. *Have resource to* is a common error.

However, *resort* is also a verb, and *resort to* is more common than *have resort to* (which some commentators refuse to allow) as in *He had to resort to trickery*. There is a difference worth noting in that *resort to* has negative overtones of *fall back on* whereas *have recourse to* has neutral or positive ones of simply *turn to*.

One way of simplifying things is to avoid *resource* as a singular, except perhaps in its special sense of *ingenuity* or *initiative — A person of resource —* though *resourcefulness* is more common. The plural *resources* is a useful word, unlikely to invite confusion with the other two.

re-cover, recover
> *re-cover*: cover again.
> *recover*: regain.

recumbent: see **incumbent**.

recuperate: see **recoup**.

redoubtable, undoubted, indubitable

> *redoubtable*: to be feared; worthy of respect.
> *undoubted*: undisputed.
> *indubitable*: incapable of being doubted.

In effect the second two are interchangeable, often resulting in the non-existent forms *undoubtable* and *undoubtably*.

redound: see **rebound** and **resound**.

reduce: see **minimise**.

refer: see **allude**.

reference, testimonial, testimony When someone applies for a job he usually has to provide a *reference* or *references* – the name(s) of somebody willing to supply information about the applicant's worth and experience. Such a person is normally called a *referee* and what he writes, normally in confidence, is also a *reference*. A *testimonial* is a similar document but an open one: that is, it is supplied to the applicant openly by his previous employer or by someone else who knows him, and the applicant may include it with his application. *Testimony* is a declaration of fact: the word is chiefly used in a legal sense to mean *evidence*.

reflective, reflexive *Reflexive* is used only in grammar, of identity between subject and object: in *He hurt himself* the verb is used reflexively and *himself* is a reflexive pronoun. *Reflective* means *capable of reflecting* (e.g. light or sound waves), *caused by reflection* or, more usually, *thoughtful, given to contemplation*.

re-form, reform

> *re-form*: form anew.
> *reform*: change in order to improve.

refurbish, refurnish

> *refurbish*: renovate.
> *refurnish*: provide new furniture for.

refute, deny *Refute* means *prove* (somebody or something) *to be wrong* (or untrue, incorrect, etc.). *Deny* means *state* (somebody, something) *to be wrong*, etc.

If a politician, accused of planning something unpopular, replies *I refute that*, he makes no sense. He has to prove his point before he can be said to have refuted anything. What he probably means is *I deny that*, but being in a tight corner he feels that the fancier *refute* sounds less defensive.

The two words are not synonymous, and *refute* cannot be used in the absence of evidence that *proves* something untrue.

regal, royal   If someone has a *regal* expression/tone of voice/air, etc., it is kingly or queenly. *Royal* is more general – *pertaining to royalty (a royal wedding)* or, by transference, *superior in size, quality*, etc. (*We received royal entertainment*).

regretful, regrettable, regretfully, regrettably

> *regretful*:   full of regret; feeling sorry.
> *regrettable*:   to be regretted.

The adverbial form *regrettably* can be used in a general sense to mean *It is unfortunate that* . . . or *We regret that* . . . , but *regretfully* should not be used in that sense, as it often is. *Regrettably, the storm caused a lot of damage* makes sense. *Regretfully, the storm caused a lot of damage* does not, because a storm cannot feel regret. *Regretfully, I have to say no* is fine.

reign, rein   A *rein* controls or guides a horse; figuratively we talk of *the reins of government*, giving *free rein to one's imagination* or keeping *a tight rein on spending*. The fact that all these have to do with the exercise of power may tempt the unwary into using *reign* – another sort of dominance, but a quite different idea, that of ruling like a sovereign (*reign of terror, chaos reigned, reigning champion*).

reiterate, iterate, repeat   Unexpectedly, *reiterate* and *iterate* mean exactly the same (*say or do again*) but in practice *reiterate* is used only of things that are said, not done, again (e.g. statements, requests) and *iterate* is hardly used at all. *Repeat* is the general word.

relation, relative   A person to whom one is related may be a *relation* or a *relative*. The only difference is that one word is preferred to the other in certain common expressions (*We are the poor relations in the family* but *He is a distant relative*). Some argue that *relation* is slightly the more common, and that it tends to be applied to closer family, but it is hard to say.

See **relationship**.

relationship, relation   Both mean *the state of being related or connected*. Generally they are interchangeable but *relation* usually has to do with the fact of a connection and *relationship* with its degree or nature.

relative

Relation (usually in the plural) is preferred if the sense is *dealings*: the *relations* between management and workers; labour *relations*; his *relations* with his neighbour. *Relationship* is preferred in the more general sense: *What is her relationship with him? A brother-sister relationship. The relationship between life and art.*

In modern terminology *relations* is a common euphemism for sexual intercourse, and a *relationship* (as in *We're having a relationship*) is an emotional or sexual affair.

relative: see **relation**.

relegate: see **delegate**.

remediable, remedial

remediable: able to be corrected, remedied, relieved, etc.
remedial: able to correct, remedy, redress, etc.
Thus a problem that is *remediable* needs *remedial* action.

renegade, renege

renegade (noun):   traitor, rebel, outlaw.
renege (verb):   go back (on one's word).
The second syllable of *renege* is the stressed one, rhyming with *vague*.

repairable, reparable   Both mean *capable of being repaired*. *Repairable* (pronounced with the stress on the second syllable) is usually applied to physical things such as a torn dress or a pair of shoes whereas *reparable* (stressed on the first syllable) is applied to abstractions such as a loss or a breach in relations.

The negatives are *unrepairable* and the familiar *irreparable*.

repeat: see **reiterate**.

repeated, repetitious, repetitive   Something that is *repeated* is said or done again (and again): *repeated ringing of the bell*. If it is *repetitive* it is overmuch repeated: *repetitive jokes* are not the same jokes but similar jokes which are wearisome because insistent, and *repetitive work* is the same work or type of work repeated in a boring way. *Repetitious* implies not only tedious but unnecessary repetition.

repel, repulse   It does not matter which of these verbs is used when the meaning is *drive back or away physically*: one may *repel* or *repulse* an attack, for example. In the more general and non-physical sense, to *repel* is to drive away by causing disgust, aversion or distaste (*His*

158

attitudes repelled them) and to *repulse* is to to drive away with coldness, discourtesy or denial (*She repulsed his advances*).

See **repellent**.

repellent, repugnant, repulsive All three mean *causing aversion*; their differences are largely ones of degree. *Repulsive* is the strongest word, suggesting physical disgust or recoil. *Repellent* is slightly milder, suggesting strong distaste. *Repugnant* is the mildest, and is often used of intellectual aversion (*repugnant idea*), but it still suggests strong dislike.

repertory, repertoire A *repertoire* consists of all the works that a performer or group of performers is competent to perform. The word is equally applied to a person's range of accomplishments: a tennis player's *repertoire of strokes* is his total stock.

Repertory means exactly the same, and could be used in all these contexts, though the foreign sound and spelling of *repertoire* commend it specially to the arts (*the conventional orchestral repertoire*). *Repertory* is the usual word, however, for a theatre or theatre company offering a number of plays for a limited number of performances instead of a single play for a long run.

repetitious: see **repeated**.

repetitive: see **repeated**.

replace, substitute These are frequently mis-used.
> *replace*:   take the place of (normally *replace by* or *with*).
> *substitute*:   put in the place of (normally *substitute for*).

Correct forms: *Central heating has replaced coal fires. People have replaced coal fires with central heating. People have substituted central heating for coal fires.*

Incorrect forms : *People have substituted coal fires with central heating. Coal fires have been substituted by central heating. Central heating has substituted coal fires.*

The football commentator's familiar *X has been substituted* (i.e. taken off the field and replaced) is wrong.

replica, duplicate A *replica* is normally something constructed as an exact copy (*replica of a Viking ship*) often on a smaller scale. A *duplicate* is any identical copy.

Duplicate is also a verb meaning *reproduce*. *Replicate* is a fancier alternative and also the correct word, on the rare occasions when it is needed, for *make a replica*.

repository

In practice, *replica* and *duplicate* (as a noun) are used interchangeably, *duplicate* the more frequently.

repository: see **depositary**.

reprehend: see **apprehend**.

repress: see **suppress**.

reproach: see **rebuke**.

repugnant: see **repellent**.

repulse: see **repel**.

repulsive: see **repellent**.

requirement, requisite A *requirement* is something imposed as a condition or obligation (*university entrance requirements*); the plural may carry the singular sense of *need* (*does not meet my requirements*).

It can also mean *something needed*, and in this sense there is nothing to choose between it and *requisite* (*Keyboard skills are a requirement/requisite in this job*), though *requisite* is usual when the thing needed is physical (*toilet requisites*).

Only *requisite* is an adjective meaning *indispensable* (*requisite skills, requisite payment*).

See **perquisite**.

reserve, preserve A *reserve* is something set aside for future use (*reserves of money*) or some stretch of land, usually public, set aside for a special purpose (*a nature reserve*).

A *preserve* is a special sphere of activity (*gambling is the preserve of fools*) or an area where game or fish is reared for (usually private) sport.

re-sign, resign
> *re-sign:* sign again.
> *resign:* give up.

resort: see **recourse**.

resound, redound Associations with success, as well as similarities in sound, sometimes result in confusion between these two. *Resound* is literally *re-echo, reverberate, produce a ringing sound* and hence *be or become widely renowned*. *Redound* is usually heard in *redound to one's credit* (i.e. contribute to one's good name). The two words are not related.

See **rebound**.

160

resource: see **recourse**.

respectable, respectful, respective
    respectable: worthy of respect.
    respectful: showing respect.
    respective: of or relating to each of several people or things.
    Respective is often used redundantly (*They all sat down in their respective places*) or incorrectly : in *He won prizes for marrows and cabbages respectively* and *The two players have a high regard for their respective skills* the required words are *both* and *each other's* (respectively).

responsive, responsible
    responsive: responding (replying, reacting) well to an influence (e.g. suggestion, statement, problem).
    responsible: holding or showing responsibility; having authority or duty; being answerable for one's actions; capable of rational conduct; trustworthy, etc.
    A *responsive* pupil reacts positively to teaching: a *responsible* one can be relied on to do conscientiously or sensibly what he has to do.

restive, restless The primary meaning of *restive* is *impatient of or resistant to control, discipline or authority;* that of *restless* is *unable to stay still or quiet. Restive* behaviour may show some of the signs of restlessness – uneasiness, anxiety, nervousness or worry, for example – but *restive* should not be used unless the idea of rebelliousness or disobedience, however mild, is present, nor should it be used, as it often is, as an alternative to *restless*.

restraint: see **constraint**.

resumé, précis Except in the USA, where a *resumé* is a brief statement of a person's qualifications and achievements, as used in job applications for instance, the difference between these two words is that a *précis* is a methodical condensed version, in the form of a summary of essential points, of something written or spoken, whereas a *resumé* is a concise account or descriptive summary, e.g. of events. In practice, *resumé* is sometimes used in place of *précis*, but not vice versa.

retort, riposte Both are a quick sharp reply, but *retort* is the stronger, carrying an additional colouring of anger or wit.
    Both may also act as verbs with these senses: neither should be used to mean merely *reply*.

retract

retract: see **recant**.

revenge: see **avenge** and **vengeance**.

reverend, reverent, reverential
    reverend: deserving reverence.
    reverent: showing or feeling reverence.
    reverential: showing (but not necessarily feeling) reverence; of the sort associated with reverence.

Reverend is normally found in the title of clergymen below the rank of Dean. Convention demands that it is followed by a Christian name or an initial or *Mr* and a surname: to refer to someone as the *Reverend Jones*, though common in America and increasingly common in Britain, is still not standard. Nor is the use of *reverend* on its own (*Good morning, Reverend*) or in the salutation of a letter: *Dear Reverend Mr Smith* should be *Dear Mr Smith* or *Dear Vicar*, etc. A letter should be addressed to (The) Rev(d). *John* or *J.* or *Mr Brown*.

Reverent indicates genuine reverence, but a *reverential hush/ silence/whisper/manner* may (or may not) lack reverence and be merely solemn or polite.

reverse, reversal, reversion
    reverse (noun):   the opposite (*The reverse is true*).
    reversal: the process of reversing (i.e. acting or being opposite to previous or normal condition); a change for the worse (*to suffer a reversal*).
    reversion: the process of reverting (i.e. returning to an earlier, especially a worse condition, or going back in thought or conversation).

review, revue   A *revue* is a light entertainment consisting of a number of short items such as songs and sketches. *Review* is needed in all other cases.

revolve: see **rotate**.

reward: see **award**.

ribbon, riband   A *riband* is a *ribbon* awarded as a decoration for some achievement – notably the *Blue Riband* awarded for the fastest crossing of the Atlantic by an ocean liner.

rifle, riffle   To *rifle* is to search through, especially in order to steal and carry off. To *riffle* is to flick or leaf through (papers, etc.) rapidly or cursorily, or to shuffle playing cards by separating them into two halves and mixing them by using the thumbs.

right, rightly   Among the many meanings of *right* are, when it is an adverb, *in accordance with propriety, correctness or truth* (*put it right*) and *in an appropriate way* (*did it right*). *Rightly* means the same, and other things too (e.g. *with good reason*), but it normally occurs before the verb (*He rightly believes*; *was rightly angry*) whereas *right* comes after it. In a few expressions the words are interchangeable: *If I remember right/rightly* . . . .

rigorous: see **vigorous**.

riposte: see **retort**.

rise, raise   As nouns, a *rise* is an upward movement or increase (in status, cost, intensity, salary, etc.) and a *raise* is an American term for a *rise* in salary. There is nothing wrong with *rise* in that sense, and no justification for importing an alternative.

   As a verb, *rise* cannot take an object (see **arise**): prices *rise* but one cannot *rise* prices. *Raise* must have an object: one can *raise* wages, but wages cannot just *raise*.

   See also **arise**, **raise** and **rear**.

rotate, revolve   Strictly speaking, *rotate* means *turn around on its own axis*, like a wheel, and *revolve* means *move around an axis or centre*, as the moon revolves around the earth. In practice the words are often used interchangeably in this sense. *Rotate* is invariable as *perform a set sequence of actions*, as when people *rotate* according to a duty rota, and *revolve* is invariable as *centre on* (*The discussion revolved around questions of cost*).

rotund: see **orotund**.

round, around   As adverbs and prepositions these mean the same, *round* being the traditional preference. Under American influence, *around* may well have become the more common, so much so that *round* is felt by some to be the more informal of the two except in a few expressions where it is invariable, such as *all the year round* and *fresh air will bring him round*. In the sense of *approximately*, only *around* is possible (*We are expecting around twenty guests*) but this too is creeping Americanisation, and there is nothing wrong with the more British *about*.

rouse, arouse

Except in the rather informal sense of *in existence* (*She is one of the best architects around*) there are no cases when *around* is better. *Round* is to be encouraged.

Round also, of course, exists as an adjective, a noun and a verb.

rouse, arouse   Very alike, but *rouse* is the more common, and *arouse* (with *arousal*) is the one normally used for *excite sexual feelings*.

In the sense of *stir into action*, *rouse* tends to be used for physical movement (*rouse the children*) and *arouse* for more abstract emotions or feelings (*arouse suspicion*). *Rouse* implies previous inactivity; *arouse* implies the stimulation of something already there but dormant. People tend to be *roused*, things *aroused*.

route, rout   *Route*, rhyming with *root*, is a choice of roads or a regular journey. As a verb it means *send by a particular route*.

Rout, rhyming with *out*, is a disastrous defeat or a state of confusion, often a headlong retreat. As a verb it means *disorganise*, *put to flight* or *defeat utterly*.

royal: see **regal**.

ruction, ruckus, rumpus
  ruction: violent dispute or uproar.
  ruckus: disturbance or row.
  rumpus: noisy or disruptive commotion.

Ruction is often used in the plural with a singular meaning (*There'll be ructions when he hears about this*). *Ruckus* is American, but increasingly heard. *Rumpus* is the most playful of the three words, all of which are slightly informal.

rudimentary: see **vestigial**.

rumble, rumple
  rumble: make deep continuous sound, like thunder (*train rumbling on*); find out (slang).
  rumple: crush or become crushed into folds or wrinkles (*a rumpled dress*): disarrange (*rumple the child's hair* (affectionately), *rumpled bedclothes*).

The first of these meanings of *rumple* is similar to one of the meanings of **crumple**. The second is not.

See **crumble**.

rural, rustic   The more general and neutrally toned word is *rural*, meaning *of the countryside or country life*. *Rustic* means the same, but connotes the simplicity or lack of sophistication associated with the country (*rustic pleasures*) or, in some contexts, crudeness and boorishness (*rustic manners*). A *rustic seat*, however, is simply one that is made of untrimmed branches or roughly dressed wood.

S

sacrosanct, sacred The first is an intensification of the second and thus means *very sacred*. It is used more generally than *sacred*, either because of the fondness that journalists and politicians have for intensives or because *sacred* seems to have more obviously religious connotations. Whatever the reason, *sacred* is now probably the stronger word, as a result of the over-work of the other.

sadism, masochism, sado-masochism, machismo The first three are abnormal conditions, usually sexual perversions, in which pleasure is derived from pain, humiliation or domination. *Masochism* is the enjoyment of such abuse imposed by another person (though loosely the word is used to denote enjoyment of one's own misery) whereas *sadism* is gratification by inflicting pain, physical or mental, on others. *Sado-masochism* – the hyphen is optional – is the combination of both of these conditions in one person.

Machismo is strong or exaggerated masculinity, or an assertion of it, or the need to prove it by daring action. The word is a vogue importation from Mexican Spanish, so recent that no one is yet quite sure whether the first syllable is *match* or *mack*: the former will probably prevail by analogy with the adjectival *macho*. The second syllable, stressed, is pronounced *iz*.

salon, saloon Apart from their special meanings in France and America respectively, a *salon* is a gathering of literary, artistic or political figures in the reception room of an elegant private house, or a stylish business establishment for fashion, hairdressing, etc., whereas a *saloon* is the more expensive bar in a pub (often called the *saloon bar*), or a public room on a ship, or a type of car.

salubrious, salutary
  salubrious: favourable to health.
  salutary: promoting an improvement, especially an educational or moral one.

sample

sample: see **example**.

sanction, punish Although a *sanction* is, among other things, a coercive measure or mechanism, the verb *to sanction* does not mean *punish*: it means *authorise*. A *sanction* can be an authorisation, aid or encouragement, though it is less frequently used in this sense.

sang, sung *Sang* is the normal past tense of *sing*. *Sung* cannot be described as incorrect, but even those dictionaries that allow it describe it as rare or even archaic. It is, however, the past participle: *it was sung, he had sung,* etc. Use *sang* on its own (*he sang badly*) and *sung* as part of a verb form (*they have sung*).

sanguine, sanguinary *Sanguine* means *optimistic*, though it is sometimes found in its earlier sense of *cheerful* or *energetic*. *Sanguinary* means *bloodthirsty, bloodstained* or *accompanied by bloodshed*.

sank, sunk, sunken *Sank* is the normal past tense of *sink*; *sunk* is acceptable but unusual (*They sank their differences*). *Sunk* is the past participle, used as part of the verb form : *it was sunk, they have sunk. Sunken* was formerly used in this way, but is now only adjectival: *sunken bath, sunken cheeks.*

sarcastic, sardonic A person who is *sarcastic* uses wounding or taunting language to express contempt, insult, scorn or bitterness. There is more humour or mockery in a *sardonic* person/remark/smile, etc.: the word implies disdain, cynicism or derision rather than cruelty. Irony may be a feature of both *sarcastic* and *sardonic* utterances: see **ironic**.

satiated, saturated, sated Normally applied to appetite or desire, *sated* means *fully satisfied* and *satiated* means *satisfied to the point of excess* or even of nausea as a result of excessive indulgence. *Saturated* is familiar in its sense of *thoroughly soaked* but can be used to mean *filled to capacity* as in *market saturated with products*.

satisfactory, satisfying *Satisfying* is the stronger word, meaning *gratifying* whereas *satisfactory* (depending on the context or tone of voice) can mean merely *adequate* or *acceptable* as well as *giving satisfaction*, a sense it shares with *satisfying*.

See **dissatisfied**.

saturated: see **satiated**.

savour, flavour   The *flavour* of food or drink is its taste but *savour* is the characteristic taste or smell of something. As a verb, *savour* means *relish*, and this sense is present in the extended sense of the noun – *distinctive quality adding interest or excitment. Flavour* too can be used in a more general sense of *predominant quality or atmosphere* as in *music with a Viennese flavour*.

scan: see **peruse**.

scant, scanty, skimpy   In various ways, all denote insufficiency. *Scant* (*barely sufficient* or *inadequate*) is the rarest of the three and is usually applied to abstract nouns (*with scant regard for his safety*). *Scanty* (*limited, insufficient*) is usually applied to the concrete as well as the abstract, and is often used of coverage. *Skimpy*, a slightly more informal word, can mean the same but has the particular senses of *made of too little material* or *excessively thrifty*.

scarce: see **rare**.

scenario, scene   *Scenario* was originally a word for the synopsis of a play, then was adopted as a fancy name for a film-script, and later still achieved vogue and near-cliché status as a word for an imagined or forecast sequence of events. It is now on the way to becoming a general alternative to *state of affairs*. The third usage is valid and indeed quite serviceable, despite the objections of some. The fourth is pretentious and pointless.
   Scenario does not mean the same as *scene*.

sceptic, septic   These look as if they may be pronounced in the same way, but they are not. *Sceptic* is pronounced *skeptic*, which is also the way it is spelt in America. It means a person who disbelieves or is inclined to disbelieve generally accepted doctrines or ideas; it is more usually found in the adjectival and noun forms *sceptical* and *scepticism*.
   Septic is a medical term meaning (roughly) *containing pus*.
   For **sceptical** see **cynical**.

Scot, Scotch, Scottish   The usual adjective is *Scottish*, though *Scotch* is traditional in a few expressions having to do with products – Scotch whisky, mist, broth, wool, egg, terrier, etc. A person from Scotland is a *Scot* and people generally are *Scots*; they object to being called *Scotch* or *Scotchmen*, though *Scotsman/woman* is unexceptionable.

167

scrimp

scrimp: see **skimp**.

scrub, shrubs *Scrub* is an area, usually an arid one, covered with low trees, bushes and *shrubs*: such vegetation is also known as *scrub*. A small collection of *shrubs* is, however, a shrubbery.

scull, skull *Scull* is the rowing term, *skull* the anatomical one.

scupper, scuttle Nautical terms, the first for an opening in a ship's side to allow water to drain from the decks, the second for a small hatch or its cover. *Scuttle* is also a verb meaning *sink a vessel by allowing water to flood in*. From this comes the more general meaning of *wreck* (plans, hopes, attempts, etc.). This sense is shared by *scupper*, a slang word for *put paid to*.

seasonable, seasonal

    seasonable: suitable for a season of the year: taking place at an appropriate time (*seasonable weather*).

    seasonal: dependent on, occurring at or varying with a season (*seasonal work*).

secure: see **procure**.

seminar, seminary Properly, a *seminar* is a select group of advanced students working as a class under a teacher; loosely, it has come to mean any group of whatever size or nature meeting for any educational purpose, such as discussion or the exchange of information. A *seminary* is a college for training priests (usually Roman Catholic); it used also to be a fancy name for a private school, especially one for young ladies.

sensibility, sensitivity, sensitiveness *Sensibility*, the ability to perceive and feel with delicacy, is often used in the plural to denote emotional and moral feelings generally, as when a person's sensibilities are hurt by ingratitude. *Sensitivity* is fine awareness of or responsiveness to external conditions, such as the feelings of other people, or to stimuli, such as artistic ones. *Sensitiveness* is usually touchiness.

    See **sensible**.

sensible, sensitive A *sensible* person has good sense and judgement; a *sensitive* one has sensitivity, that is, delicate feelings. *Sensitive* (to) means *readily affected* (by), often in the sense of being easily hurt, and *aware of, responsive to* (feelings, etc.).

    See **sensibility, insensate**.

168

sensual, sensuous, sensory   *Sensory* is the neutral adjective for *related to the senses*. *Sensuous* is *affecting or taking pleasure in the senses*, as one might derive *sensuous pleasure* from skiing. *Sensual* means excessively or self-indulgently gratifying the senses, especially sexually.

sentiment, sentimentality   A *sentiment* may simply be an attitude or opinion (*Those are my sentiments on the matter*) but it is more usually one tinged with emotion or inspired by feeling rather than thought (*anti-war sentiment*). In some cases *sentiment* is merely another word for emotion or feeling (*patriotic sentiment*) or an emotional significance or effect. Occasionally it means *refined feeling*.

Sentimentality may be no more than a state or act characterised by feeling (especially one of nostalgia or romance) rather than thought: an example of this usage is *did it out of sentimentality*. Generally, however, the word is used less neutrally, more disparagingly, to denote excessive or superficial feeling, or even wallowing in emotion (*a film/speech/reunion full of sentimentality*).

See **maudlin**.

septic: see **sceptic**.

sergeant, serjeant   *Sergeant* is the correct spelling, the other one being limited to a very few traditional titles such as that of the *Serjeant at Arms* in the Houses of Parliament.

sestet, sextet
    sestet: the last six lines of a sonnet.
    sextet: a set of six; a piece of music for six instruments or voices; the performers of such a piece.

sew, sow   *Sew* (fasten with needle and thread) has the past tense *sewed* and the past participle *sewn*: hence *she sewed/had sewn*. *Sow* (plant seed) has a similar pattern of *sowed* and *sown*. The past participles *sewed* and *sowed* exist but are so uncommon that they are likely to be interpreted as errors.

sewage, sewerage   *Sewage* is waste material of the kind removed in sewers. *Sewerage* is the name for its removal or for a system of sewers.

sextet: see **sestet**.

shallow, callow   When applied to a person, *shallow* means *superficial*, especially in one's feelings. *Callow* means *immature*, especially in one's attitudes.

shear, sheer   *Shear* is the verb for *cut* or *break* (*the bolt sheared off*) and the noun, often plural, for a cutting implement. *Sheer* is required in all other cases (*sheer luck/cliff*, etc.)

shew, show   *Shew* is the old form, now archaic; *show* is now invariable.

shone, shined   The verb *shine* has *shone* as its past tense and past participle (*the sun shone/has shone all day*) except when it is used with a direct object to mean *make bright by polishing*. It then has *shined* as past tense and past participle (*he shined/has shined his walking boots*).

show: see **shew**.

showed, shown   Both are past participles of *show* but *shown* is much the more usual.

shrub: see **scrub**.

shun: see **spurn**.

sick, sickly   A *sick* child is ill; a *sickly* child is inclined to be frequently ill. Both words have other meanings (*a sick joke, sick to death, a sickly smell, etc.*).

sight, site   A *site* is a piece of land; as a verb it means *locate*. *Sight* is required for all other meanings.

silicon, silicone   *Silicon* is the element found in sand and now heard so often in *silicon chip*. *Silicone* is a chemical compound with heat-resistant and water-resistant properties, used in lubricants and insulators.
The final syllable of *silicon* is pronounced *k'n*; in *silicone*, however, it is pronounced *cone*.

similar, analogous   *Analogous*, pronounced with a hard *g* despite the soft one in *analogy*, means *similar or corresponding in certain respects* and its use to mean no more than *similar* is loose.
See **analogy** and **similarly**.

similarly, correspondingly   *Similarly* does not mean *in the same way*, because *similar* denotes likeness and *same* denotes identity (compare *They lived in the same house* and *They lived in a similar house*).
similarly: in a similar way.
correspondingly: in a matching way.

Thus *If taxes are lowered, public spending will correspondingly* (not similarly) *be reduced.*

simplistic, simplified, simple *Simplistic* is often used as a showy variant of *simple*. It is not: it is a disparaging word meaning *over-simple, shallow, naive* or even *foolish*. *Simplified* means *made simpler*.

simulate: see **dissimulate**.

simultaneously: see **instantly**.

site: see **sight**.

situated, situate People are sometimes puzzled to come across *situate* in house-agents' advertisements, the only place where the word is normally found (the assumption being that it sounds grand, whereas it is merely pompous). It is a legal term; normal people use *situated*.

skilful, skilled Both mean *having skill*, and they are often used interchangeably, but there is a difference in emphasis. *Skilled* implies special training or long experience: *skilful* implies natural ability (which may, of course, be refined by practice or training). *Skilled* is specially applied to work-people; *skilful* is a more general word.

skimp, scrimp *Skimp* is normally used to mean *give insufficient attention or care to* though it can mean *be very sparing*. *Scrimp* is chiefly used of money or material goods; it means *be frugal or niggardly* (as in the expression *scrimp and save*) or *treat meanly*.

skimpy: see **scant**.

skulk, sulk To *skulk* is to move stealthily or lurk, especially from cowardice or with a sinister intention; the word is often used to mean *evade duties*. To *sulk* is to brood sullenly and silently.

skull: see **scull**.

slander: see **libel**.

sled, sledge, sleigh *Sledge* is the usual word, *sled* being chiefly North American and *sleigh* being largely reserved for popular songs and for a vehicle rather than a plaything.

sleight, slight *Sleight* is found only in *sleight of hand* (adroitness in a conjuring trick or in deception more generally). In all other cases *slight* is needed.

slippy, slippery   The Oxford Dictionary used to regard *slippy* as a 'vulgar' alternative to *slippery* though the current edition has moderated as far as 'colloquial'. Other dictionaries prefer 'informal' or 'dialect'; yet others regard it as now a fully fledged alternative to *slippery*. Idiom requires *a slippery customer* (an unreliable person) and *Look slippy* (Hurry up). In other cases it is safest to choose *slippery*.

sluggard: see **laggard**.

smelt, smelled   These are alternative forms, of which *smelt* is the more popular. *Smelt* is additionally a verb (past tense *smelted*) meaning *heat in order to extract metal from ore*.

sneak, steal   Although both can mean *move furtively or stealthily*, *sneak* has associations of guilt that *steal* lacks. The same is true when the words mean *accomplish secretly* (*sneak/steal a glance*). To *sneak* is generally to bring, take or put stealthily; to *steal* is to obtain or convey furtively. *Sneak off* means *leave unobtrusively*.

sociable, social   The first is related to the word *society* in its sense of companionship; the second is related in a more general sense.
  sociable: fond of and friendly in company.
  social: relating to society (*social problems/justice/services*).
  A *social* evening, club or circle brings one into contact with other people in society; only if it is characterised by friendliness can it be called *sociable*.
  See **unsociable**.

solid, stolid   *Stolid* describes that sort of temperament that shows little emotion: its use can range from the neutral *impassive, not easily excited* or *unemotional* to the more pejorative *obstinate* or *apparently stupid*. *Solid*, when applied to personality, means *reliable, staunch* and is a more positive word.
  See **solidarity**.

solidarity, solidity   *Solidarity* is mutual dependence among people – a unity based on community of interests, opinions and action. *Solidity* is the quality of being **solid** in all its meanings, such as when one speaks of the solidity of a substance, an article, an institution or even of an abstraction (*political party enjoying solidity in its support, etc.*).
  See **solid**.

soluble, solvable   Either will do for *capable of being solved* but only *soluble* means *capable of being dissolved*.
  See **unsolvable**.

someplace: see **somewhere**.

some time, sometime   *Some time* is either adjective + noun meaning *a certain time* (*Is there some time when I can talk to you?*) or a shortened version of *at some time* meaning *at a certain* (unstated) *time* (*He died some time ago*). *Sometime* is an adverb meaning *at some unspecified future time* (*I'll see you sometime soon*) or *at some point of time* (*I phoned him sometime last evening*). The distinction between these and the second definition of *some time* (a distinction most people ignore) is a matter of deciding whether the *some* has the sense of *certain* or not; if it has, it should be written separately.

somewhere, someplace   Children are quicker than adults at picking up Americanisms from television and incorporating them into their daily vocabulary, so perhaps when the present generation grows up the American *someplace* will become common in adult writing and speech. For the moment, its British synonym *somewhere* must be regarded as standard, and *someplace* as both informal and unnecessary.

sonorous, stentorian
>   *sonorous*:   deep, resonant (usually applied to the voice or language).
>   *stentorian*:   very loud (usually applied to the voice).

south, southern   The usage described under **north, northern** applies also to these words.

sow: see **sew**.

sparse, spare   In their sense of *scanty, meagre*, the first is used for *distributed thinly* (*sparse vegetation/population*) and the second for *lean, wiry*, usually applied to someone's build and implying good health. *Spare* can also mean *very economical* or *frugal*.

spasmodic, sporadic   Both mean *intermittent* but *spasmodic* is related to *spasm* and the implication is of periods of inactivity punctuated by unpredictable jerkiness or sudden violence of action. *Sporadic* is a more neutral word for *occurring from time to time* in a rather desultory or haphazard way. It also means *scattered* or *isolated*.

special, especial   Previously distinct, now interchangeable, with *special* very much the more common and *especial* apparently in danger of falling into disuse.
>   See **especially**.

specialism, speciality, specialty   A person's *specialism* is his particular subject of study or field of activity. *Speciality* may be used in this sense, but is usually more specific, referring to a special interest, skill, product or characteristic. *Specialty* is the American word for *speciality*, especially in the sense of *line of work*, and also exists as a legal word in British English.

See **especially**.

specious, spurious   Anything that is *specious* is seemingly correct, sound, true or attractive, but actually not so. Whatever is *spurious* is not genuine or real but invalid, counterfeit or based on mistaken ideas. There are occasions when the words come very close together (*a specious/spurious argument*) but *specious* normally implies intention to deceive whereas *spurious* generally does not.

spelled, spelt   There used to be a preference for *spelled* as the past tense (*He spelled it incorrectly*) and *spelt* as the past participle (*He has spelt it incorrectly*), though either form was acceptable, and still is, in either case. The present trend is towards *spelt* in both cases.

spilled, spilt   Either will do. Most people seem to prefer *spilt*.

spirituous, spiritous, spiritual
    spirituous: containing alcohol.
    spiritual: relating to the spirit or the soul rather than the physical body.
  Spiritous is a variant of *spirituous*.

spirt, spurt   There used to be a difference, *spurt* being a verb and noun meaning (*make*) *a short extra effort* and *spirt* or *spurt* a verb and noun meaning (*gush out in*) *a jet*. Nowadays it is customary to use *spurt* in all these senses.

splutter, sputter   These are variants and may, except for the rare scientific senses of *sputter*, be used interchangeably. A person who speaks in a hesitant, hasty, confused or disjointed way with spitting sounds or stammerings as if choking with excitement, anger, embarrassment or laughter, or who ejects bits of saliva or food in the process, is said to *splutter*. Anything that makes explosive popping sounds – a firework, hot fat, a fire ejecting sparks, for instance – is normally said to *sputter*, though *splutter* would not be wrong. Both words may also be used as nouns to denote the noise or process of spluttering/sputtering.

spoil, despoil   To *despoil* is to plunder, pillage or deprive by force, usually as an act of war. It has nothing whatsoever to do with the familiar senses of *spoil* except in *the spoils of war,* the booty, land, etc. gained by war.

spoiled, spoilt   As the past tense or past participle of *spoil* either will serve, though *spoilt* is perhaps the more common. *Spoilt* is also the more normal adjectival form (*a spoilt child*).

sporadic: see **spasmodic**.

sprain, strain   A *sprain* is an injury of a joint, often ankle or wrist, by sudden twisting or wrenching of ligaments, resulting in pain, swelling and temporary disability. A *strain* is more general – any injury or damage caused by over-exertion, as one may *strain* a muscle or one's back.
　　Both words are also verbs.

sprint, spurt   A *sprint* is any quick run or race. A burst of speed at the end of a long run may be a *sprint* or a *spurt*. A *spurt* is also any short burst of effort, or a sudden gush or jet; as a verb it means *show a sudden burst of energy, speed or activity* or *gush out in a jet*.
　　See **spirt**.

spurious: see **specious**.

spurn, shun
　　spurn: reject with contempt.
　　shun: avoid deliberately, usually habitually.

spurt: see **spirt** and **sprint**.

sputter: see **splutter**.

stable, staple   Because of its familiarity, *stable* (*steady, firm, lasting*, etc.) is sometimes wrongly used in place of the less common *staple*, which means *principal* or *constantly used* and is commonly found in such expressions as *staple food/commodity/product*: a *staple diet* is one principally based on a particular and popular food.

stalactite, stalagmite   A *stalactite* is a body of calcium carbonate hanging, rather like an icicle, from the roof of a cave or cavern; think of something holding *tight*. A *stalagmite* is a similar deposit, also formed by dripping or trickling water, but projecting from the floor of a cave.

stammer, stutter Both of these may be speech defects, a *stammer* being characterised by hesitations, repetitions and stops, and a *stutter* by the recurring repetition of consonants, especially initial ones. The words may be used more generally to describe hesitant or confused speech (for instance, under the stress of confusion or fear) either as nouns or verbs.

stanch, staunch *Stanch* is usually found as a verb meaning *stop the flow* (especially of blood from a wound). *Staunch* can mean the same, but it is normally used as an adjective meaning *steadfast* (in loyalty, principle, etc.).

The *a* in *stanch* is pronounced as in *father*, but *staunch* rhymes with *launch*.

staple: see **stable**.

stationary, stationery Commonly confused. *Stationary* is the adjective (think of *a* for adjective in the ending) meaning *not moving*. *Stationery* is the noun for writing materials.

statutory: see **mandatory**.

staunch: see **stanch**.

steal: see **sneak**.

stentorian: see **sonorous**.

sticker, stickler

     sticker: person who is persevering and industrious.
     stickler: person who insists on exactness or close attention to detail, especially in an observance or formality.

stile: see **style**.

stimulant, stimulus Both signify an incentive, something that arouses one to activity, but in practice *stimulant* is usually reserved for a drug that produces a temporary increase in an organism's activity. *Stimulus* is the more general word (*competition acting as a stimulus*); its plural is *stimuli*, the final syllable pronounced *-lie* or *-lee*.

stoic, stoical There is no difference in meaning (*impassive, resigned*, especially in showing no feeling in suffering) but there is a slight preference for using *stoic* before a noun (*stoic indifference*) and *stoical* after a verb (*remained stoical*).

stolid: see **solid**.

storey, story   *Storey* (plural *storeys*) is the English word for a floor of a building; the American spelling is *story* (plural *stories*) which in English is reserved for *tale*. The adjectival forms are either *three-storeyed* (etc.) or *three-storey*, the latter being more common.

strain: see **sprain**.

strait, straight   As an adjective, *strait* (meaning *narrow*) is archaic and found only in a couple of expressions deriving from Matthew VII, 14 (*strait and narrow*, *strait is the gate*, the former meaning *the strictly moral way*) and in *strait-jacket* and *strait-laced*. As a noun it is usually found in the plural with a singular meaning to signify a narrow stretch of water between two larger ones (*Straits of Gibraltar*) or a state of perplexity or difficulty (*dire straits*). It has nothing to do with the familiar meanings of *straight*.

   The straight and narrow is probably now more common than the more Biblical *strait and narrow*. The spelling *straight-jacket* and *straight-laced* have also come to be regarded as acceptable, though they are more obviously wrong. All three expressions have to do with tightness, not straightness.

strata: see **stratum**.

strategy, strategem, tactics   Whatever some dictionaries may say, the first two are quite distinct:

   strategy: the art or science of planning and conducting a military campaign or other large enterprise to achieve a goal.

   strategem: plan or trick intended to deceive.

   tactics: the art or skill of disposing forces in combat or deploying resources or procedures to accomplish an end.

   In general terms a *strategy* is a policy or master-plan, and *tactics* are the means of bringing it to fruition.

stratosphere: see **atmosphere**.

stratum, strata   *Strata* is the plural of *stratum* (*a distinct layer or level*). *Stratums* is possible but unusual; *stratas* is illiterate. *Strata* is increasingly found as a singular (*This strata of society is. . .*) but this must be ascribed to carelessness or ignorance.

stricken: see **struck**.

stringed, strung   *Stringed* is an adjective (*stringed instrument*). *Strung* is the past tense and past participle of the verb *string* as in *highly strung*.
>   *stringed*:   having strings.
>   *strung*:   provided with strings; suspended, stretched; tensed.

strove, striven, strived   *Strived* is found in the Bible and elsewhere, and is still sometimes heard (perhaps by analogy with *dived, hived, arrived*, etc.), but it is wrong. The past tense of *strive* is *strove* (*However hard he strove. . . .*) and the past participle *striven* (*he had striven to. . .*) not *strove*.

struck, stricken   The archaic past participle of *strike, stricken* survives in a number of expressions such as *a stricken ship, grief-stricken* and a few others, with the adjectival sense of *distressed*, but the normal past participle is *struck* (*I was struck dumb*).

strung: see **stringed**.

stupor, torpor   Both denote a state of reduced activity, mental and physical. *Stupor* is most usually the state induced by drugs or shock — one of near-unconsciousness and dulled sense of feeling, especially of the senses. *Torpor* is apathy or sluggishness, especially of a physical kind.

stutter: see **stammer**.

style, stile   Apart from its technical use in the language of architecture, *stile* is found only when denoting a set of steps for getting over a wall or fence. *Style* is required in all other senses.

subconscious: see **unconscious**.

subliminal, sublime, sublimated
>   *subliminal*:   functioning below the level of sensation or conscious awareness.
>   *sublime*:   noble, elevated, perfect; inspiring awe.
>   *sublimated*:   refined or modified from a primitive to a socially acceptable form.

submerge: see **immerse**.

subnormal: see **abnormal**.

subsequent: see **consequent**.

substantial, substantive   Although both can mean *real, true, solid in foundation*, these words are usually distinguished in everyday use. *Substantial* means *having considerable size, wealth, value or importance* and should not be used, as it often is, as an impressive substitute for merely *large*. *Substantive* means *relating to the essential nature of something* (as in *substantive discussions/progress*). It is also a technical word meaning *permanent* (as distinct from acting or temporary) as when the appointment of an army corporal, say, who has been acting in that rank but not paid accordingly is made *substantive*.

substitute: see **replace**.

succeed, follow
> *follow*:   go or come after (often in a physical sense).
> *succeed*:   come next in order (after someone or something) and take the place of.

The words are not synonyms.

See **consecutive**.

successive: see **consecutive**.

succubus: see **incubus**.

sufferance, suffering, suffrage
> *sufferance*:   tolerance (as implied by lack of objection). *On sufferance* means *tolerated with reluctance*.
> *suffering*:   subjection to pain.
> *suffrage*:   the right to vote; the exercise of that right.

suit, suite   Both mean *group*. A *suit* (rhymes with *root* or *cute*) is a set of clothes or cards; a *suite* (pronounced *sweet*) is a set of furniture, rooms, attendants or musical pieces. Only *suit* is additionally a verb.

sulk: see **skulk**.

summary, paraphrase, summation
> *summary*:   brief account covering the main points of something.
> *paraphrase*:   restatement (of text, passage, etc.) in other words.
> *summation*:   process of forming a sum; a total; cumulative effect.

The last of these is sometimes confused with the first by those who attach more importance to sound than sense. A *summation* is an adding together: a *summary* is a reduction. *Summation* is best left to mathematicians.

summon, summons To *summon* is to order to come; to *summons* is to order to appear in court, though *summon* may be used in this sense too. Only *summons* is a noun, however, denoting an authoritative order to appear, or a legal requirement to attend a court.

sung: see **sang**.

sunk, sunken: see **sank**.

superficial, superfluous That which is *superficial* is on the surface, lacking depth; that which is *superfluous* is more than enough.

supersede, surpass

> *supersede*: take the place of.
> *surpass*: be greater or better than.

When something or someone *supersedes* another it is often because of its or his superiority, but that should not imply that the words are synonymous.

supine: see **prone**.

supplement: see **complement**.

suppress, repress Both mean *exclude* (e.g. a thought or feeling) *from one's mind*, but *suppress* implies that this is done consciously whereas *repress* implies that it is done by psychological inhibitions. Both also mean *put down by force*, but again there is a difference, *suppress* implying abolition (*suppress a riot/publication/the truth*), *repress* implying holding in harsh check (*repress a religious sect*).

surpass: see **supersede**.

suspicious, suspect Only *suspicious* can mean *distrustful* (*was suspicious of the salesman's claims for the product*). Both *suspicious* and *suspect* can mean *arousing suspicion* (*circumstances of his death were suspicious*) but *suspect* has the special meaning of *arousing suspicion about quality*, as in *The ship's design is suspect*.

As an adjective *suspect* is stressed on the first syllable; as a verb it is stressed on the second.

swam, swum *I swam* and *I have/had swum*, always.

swot, swat

> *swot*: study intensively. Also noun, one who does this.
> *swat*: hit sharply (especially to kill insect).

The first is informal as a noun, rather less so as a verb.

180

swum: see **swam**

sympathy, empathy These are not synonyms. *Empathy* has a restricted meaning : it is the capacity for deep understanding of another's feelings to the extent of imaginative participation in them; it is also the attribution of one's own feelings to a work of art (e.g. a piece of music). *Sympathy* implies less intimacy or identification: it is an inclination to feel (or think) like another person, or an understanding or sharing of his emotions, especially when showing pity or compassion.

synonymous, analogous Both have to do with sameness: a synonym has identity with something else; an analogy merely has similarity in a number of respects, others being different.

> *synonymous* (with): meaning the same (or nearly the same) as; being another name for; strongly suggestive of (*Capitalism is synonymous with self-interest*).
>
> *analogous* (to): capable of being compared to, or similar or corresponding, in some respects (*Capitalism is analogous to communism in its lack of humanity*).

Note that *analogous* is pronounced with a hard *g* as in *get*, and *analogy* with a soft one as in *gesture*.

T

tactics: see **strategy**.

tasteful, tasty
> *tasteful*: showing good taste.
> *tasty*: having a pleasant flavour.

taught, taut *Taut* is the adjective meaning *tightly stretched*, *tensed* or *stressed*. *Taught* is the past tense and past participle of *teach*.

teach: see **learn**.

teeter, totter *Teeter* mainly occurs in the expression *teeter on the brink*: the sense is that of swaying from side to side, as if in doubt as to whether to plunge in or not, or as if in danger of falling. The word can mean *move* *unsteadily*, but *totter* is more usual in this sense. *Totter* also means *to be unstable, ready to collapse* (*prop up a tottering economy*).

temerity, timidity   Despite their apparent similarity, these are near-opposites.

>   *temerity*:   rashness, boldness, foolhardiness, unreasonable disregard for danger.
>   *timidity*:   lack of boldness or self-confidence; shyness, fear; capacity to be easily upset.

See **timid**.

temporal, temporary

>   *temporal*:   relating to time (as opposed to space, eternity, etc.) or to the secular (as opposed to the spiritual).
>   *temporary*:   lasting for a limited time.

tenacity, pertinacity   *Pertinacity* is doggedness in opinion or purpose; the word tends to be used disparagingly to imply unreasonable or inconvenient obstinacy. *Tenacity* is used rather admiringly, and has a more general sense of holding firmly, retaining or sticking, both literally and figuratively.

tendency: see **trend**.

tepid, vapid

>   *tepid*:   moderately warm; unenthusiastic.
>   *vapid*:   insipid; without liveliness, strength or interest; boring, dull.

A *vapid* speech may well be greeted by *tepid* applause.

terminus, terminal   *Terminus* is the normal word for a station at the end (or beginning) of a bus or railway route. *Terminal*, adopted by airlines as the name for a building acting as an access point to aircraft and their routes, shows signs of ousting it. *Terminal* has several other meanings, notably in the languages of computing and electricity.

   The plural of *terminus* may be *terminuses* or *termini* (final syllable pronounced as *eye*).

testimonial: see **reference**.

testimony: see **reference**.

testy, tetchy   *Tetchy* means *irritable* or *peevish*. The less common word *testy* is less disparaging: it means *impatient* and implies that the ill-humour or anger is more justified. But there is very little to choose between the two words.

thesis, treatise   A *thesis* is a piece of written work embodying original research, submitted as a requirement for a degree or diploma, and thus to be examined or defended. A *treatise*, more generally, is any formal written exposition on a subject, especially dealing with its principles; it will embody the writer's thoughts but not necessarily any research.

though: see **although**.

thrash, thresh   Plunging about in a wild manner, a drowning man or a person enmeshed in an argument may either *thrash* or *thresh* around. Only *thrash*, however, can mean *flog* or *defeat*, and only *thresh* can mean *beat grain from corn*. To *thrash out* is to discuss exhaustively in order to reach a solution.

thrilling, enthralling   Both words express extreme pleasure but of different quality. *Thrilling* implies piercing, tingling, quivering: a thrill is a shiver of feeling or emotion. *Enthralling* implies a deeper, perhaps more thoughtful and prolonged and less emotional delight: to be enthralled is to be held spellbound.

till, until   Interchangeable, though *until* is slightly more formal, *till* being more common in speech. As the first word in a sentence, *until* is perhaps the more popular, even in speech.

   Until tends to gather redundant words around itself: *up until*, *until such time as* and *unless and until* mean no more than *until* on its own.

timid, timorous   These are very close and often mean the same, but whereas *timid* is normally used to indicate self-effacement, especially in human relationships, *timorous* implies a more marked shrinking back in fear or apprehension.

   See **temerity**.

timidity: see **temerity**.

timorous: see **timid**.

titillate, titivate   To *titillate* is to stimulate or excite pleasantly. To *titivate* is to make oneself spruce or smarten something up. Both have a jocular feel, and *titivate* especially is often used rather disparagingly, as if the attempt to prettify were pretentious or unsuccessful.

   An alternative spelling *tittivate* is possible but unnecessary.

tire, tyre   For the rubber ring placed over the rim of a wheel, only *tyre* is the acceptable spelling in British English, though the older form *tire* is invariable in American English. In Britain *tire* means *weary*.

toilet, toilette   One's *toilet* may be the act of dressing and grooming oneself, though the word is seldom used in this sense, except perhaps jocularly, because of the associations of its far more common meaning. *Toilette*, pronounced in the French way, is a formal but even rarer alternative.

tolerance, toleration
> *tolerance*:   the capacity to tolerate.
> *toleration*:   the act of tolerating.

In practice, *tolerance* is used in both of these senses, and *toleration* is reserved to denote the freedom to hold views, notably religious ones, that are different from the normal ones in a culture.

Intolerance acts as the opposite of both words.

ton, tonne, tun   These sound alike, rhyming with *sun*.
> *ton*:   a unit of weight (2240 pounds).
> *tonne*:   a unit of weight (1000 kilograms or 2204.6 pounds). Also known as a metric ton.
> *tun*:   a large cask.

torpor: see **stupor**.

tortuous, torturous
> *tortuous*:   having many twists, bends or turns (*a tortuous route*); involved or devious (*a tortuous argument*).
> *torturous*:   causing torture, pain or anguish (*a torturous relationship*).

The most common error is one of mispronunciation. Because *torture* is a common word, people often say *torturous* when they mean *tortuous*, as in *The negotiations were torturous*. Perhaps inadvertently, they are often right: things that are *tortuous* are often wearing and *torturous*. But in practice *torturous* is seldom used intentionally: instead of *It was a torturous experience* people are more likely to say *It was torture*.

totter: see **teeter**.

towards, toward, untoward   *Towards* is the normal preposition, *toward* being a little used alternative. *Untoward* means *unfavourable*, *unseemly*, *unfortunate*, *perverse* and usually occurs after such words as *anything*, *nothing* and *something*.

trace, vestige Both mean *evidence of something that has existed or happened* but a *vestige* is smaller than a *trace* and may be minute. Another useful shade of meaning is that a *vestige* is evidence of something that no longer exists. A person who disappears *without trace* may still be alive.

transcendent, transcendental These share the general sense of *surpassing ordinary limits of experience* and therefore sometimes overlap. Usually, however, *transcendent* is used to mean *pre-eminent* and *transcendental* to mean *mystical, visionary*, though both have special senses, mainly in philosophy and theology.

transient, transitory Only the finest distinction separates these two, which mean *lasting for a short time*. *Transient* tends to imply rapid (physical) movement, and *transitory* rapid disappearance (*a transient population, transitory happiness*) but to all intents and purposes the words are interchangeable.

translucent, transparent Compared with something that is *transparent*, something *translucent* allows light to pass through only partially or diffusely, so that objects beyond cannot be distinctly seen. Roughly, then, *translucent* means *semi-transparent*.

transport, transportation, deportation In the sense of *means or system of transporting* and *the act of transporting or being transported* the usual British term is *transport* and *transportation* the usual American one. Choose the shorter word.

Transportation is, however, the correct term for the enforced conveyance of offenders to a penal colony. *Deportation* can mean the same but, as its prefix implies, the proper sense of the word is *expulsion* (e.g. of unwanted aliens) *from a country*.

treachery, treason Both mean *betrayal*, especially of trust, but *treason* has the special sense of betrayal of one's sovereign or country. In everyday speech *treason* is used as a more powerful version of *treachery* in a figurative (and sometimes jocular) sense to denote insubordinate questioning or defiance of policy or ethos in an organisation.

treatise: see **thesis**.

treble, triple As a general rule *treble* is used, as an adjective, to mean *three times as many* (as in the football pools' *treble chance*) and *triple* to mean *having three parts* (as in the athlete's *triple jump*), but this distinction is not invariable and the words are often used inter-

185

changeably. They are synonymous as verbs (*increase threefold*) and nouns (*a threefold amount* or *a group of three*).

Treble has another range of meanings, mostly related to music, that have nothing to do with *triple*.

trend, tendency   A *trend* is an actual movement (*the trend in house prices*). A *tendency* is an inclination to move or do something (*house prices showing a tendency to increase*). In other words, a *trend* is something that is happening; a *tendency* is a propensity or predisposition towards a certain sort of action.

trillion: see **billion**.

triple: see **treble**.

triumphant, triumphal

> *triumphant*:   victorious (*triumphant team*); rejoicing in victory or success (*triumphant celebration*).
>
> *triumphal*:   having to do with the commemoration or celebration of a victory (*triumphal procession/arch/progress/march*).

Triumphal has the more formal and restricted meaning.

troop, troupe, trooper, trouper   A *troupe* is a group of actors or other performers, especially one that travels. The word is also a verb (*travel in a group of performers*) and gives rise to *trouper*, a seasoned and reliable performer or helper. A *trooper*, however, is a cavalry soldier.

A *troop* is a body of people (especially scouts and cavalry) or animals. *Troops* are soldiers. To *troop* is to gather or move in a group, especially a regimented one.

troubled, troublesome

> *troubled*:   experiencing trouble.
>
> *troublesome*:   giving trouble.

troupe: see **troop**.

tumult, turmoil   Both signify commotion, violent agitation and confused movement, but *tumult* normally implies noise. *Turmoil*, the more familiar word, is often used of emotional upheaval or of turbulent disagreements or discontent within a society or group – not necessarily noisy or riotous ones, as *tumult* suggests.

tun: see **ton**.

turgid, turbid
> *turgid*: swollen, distended; (of language) pompous, inflated, laboured.
>
> *turbid*: in turmoil; thick, dense, muddy (*turbid river*).
>
> For **turmoil** see **tumult**.

turmoil: see **tumult**.

tyre: see **tire**.

U

unable, incapable *Incapable* denotes permanent lack of ability; *unable* denotes lack of ability in specific circumstances. *I am unable to sing* means that I can sing but am prevented; *I am incapable of singing* means that I cannot under any circumstances.

unaffected, disaffected The first is the opposite of *affected* (i.e. not altered, moved or influenced) and also means *without affectation, genuine*. To be *disaffected*, however, is to be discontented, alienated and resentful, especially towards authority.

unapproachable: see **irreproachable**.

unaware, oblivious, unawares It comes as a surprise to many to learn that *oblivious* should be followed by *of* and means *forgetful (of)*. It is more usually found followed by *to* as if it meant *not conscious of* or *unaware*; it does not (though the usage will doubtless prevail in time) and careful users of the language will avoid the error.

Unaware is an adjective meaning *not aware, ignorant of*. *Unawares* is an adverb meaning *unexpectedly, by surprise* as in *The storm caught them unawares*.

unbelief: see **disbelief**.

unbeliever: see **disbeliever**.

unconscious, subconscious The *unconscious* is that part of the mind of which we are not aware (i.e. it has ideas, impulses and instincts we cannot analyse) but which affects behaviour. The *subconscious* is that part of which we are only partly aware. Whatever the importance of the distinction in the language of psychology, it is immaterial for everyday purposes: for most people, to do something *unconsciously* is not to know that one is doing it; to do something *subconsciously* is not to know why one is doing it.

underlay, underlie

> *underlay*:   lay or place underneath (something); provide (something) with support.
>
> *underlie*:   lie under; be the basis of.

For the complexities of *lay* and *lie* see **lie**. *Underlay*, a little-used verb, has *underlaid* in the past tenses. *Underlie* has *underlay* as the past tense and *underlain* as the past participle. Thus *The turf needs underlaying/to be underlaid with sand; Mutual suspicion underlies/underlay/has underlain diplomatic relations between the two countries.*

undertone: see **overtone**.

undiscriminating: see **indiscriminate**.

undoubted: see **redoubtable**.

uneatable: see **eatable**.

unequivocal, unequivocable   The first means *clear*, *unambiguous*. The second, however frequently heard, simply does not exist and is an *unequivocal* illiteracy.

unethical: see **amoral**.

unexceptional, unexceptionable

> *unexceptional*:   normal, commonplace, ordinary; subject to no exceptions.
>
> *unexceptionable*: unobjectionable, beyond criticism.

If a person's behaviour is *unexceptional* there is nothing out of the ordinary about it. If it is *unexceptionable* it is irreproachable.

See also **exceptional**.

unexplained, inexplicable   To say that something is *unexplained* implies that it may have an explanation but that the explanation has not been given. Something that is *inexplicable*, however, has no explanation.

unforeseen, unforeseeable   *Unforeseen* circumstances are those that can be foreseen but are not. *Unforeseeable* ones cannot be foreseen. What are often described as *unforeseen circumstances* are, strictly speaking, *unforeseeable* ones.

uninterested: see **disinterested**.

unlawful: see **illegal**.

unorganised, disorganised In the sense of *lacking organisation or the ability to organise* either will do; a person who has messy work–habits may be described as *unorganised* or *disorganised*. More strictly, *unorganised* is applied to anything that is not organised, and *disorganised* is the general term for *lacking coherence*. An unorganised rebellion may nonetheless be very effective; a disorganised one is unlikely to be.

unpractical: see **impracticable**.

unproven: see **proven**.

unreadable: see **illegible**.

unrepairable: see **repairable**.

unsatisfied: see **dissatisfied**.

unsociable, unsocial, antisocial

> *unsociable*: not inclined to associate with others.
>
> *unsocial*: not social. Usually found in *unsocial hours* which are working hours outside the conventional working day and which therefore may merit extra pay.
>
> *antisocial*: opposed to the good of society. *Antisocial behaviour* is selfish or self-seeking.

Antisocial is a strong and useful word which is weakened if used to mean no more than *unfriendly* or *unsociable*, as it often is.

See **sociable**.

unsolvable, insolvable, insoluble All mean *not capable of being solved*. *Insolvable* is rare (not all dictionaries admit it) and chiefly American. There is nothing to choose between the other two: *insoluble* is the more frequent and has the additional meaning *not capable of being dissolved*.

until: see **till**.

untoward: see **toward**.

unused: see **disused**.

unwonted, unwanted

> *unwonted*: out of the ordinary (*day of unwonted heat*).
>
> *unwanted*: not wanted.

The second syllable of *unwonted* rhymes with *don't*.

upward, upwards   *Upward* is adjective (*upward mobility*) and adverb (*look upward*). *Upwards*, which means the same, is only an adverb, and probably used more often than *upward*.

urban, urbane

> *urban*:   relating to a city or town (*urban decay*).
> *urbane*:   characterised by sophistication; polite or smooth in manner (*urbane wit*).

The first is stressed on the first syllable, the second on the last, which is pronounced to rhyme with *lane*.

use, usage   Careful writers discriminate between *use* (the act of using, as in *put to good use*) and *usage* (the way or customary manner in which something is used, as in *English usage*) though there are many cases when such distinction is irrelevant (*car has been subjected to rough use/usage*).

See **utilise**.

utilise, use   Generally used interchangeably, the longer word being preferred by the pretentious. Careful usage favours *use* for *put into action or service* and *utilise* for the more restricted *make practical, productive or worthwhile use of*. When such a distinction is not possible, choose the shorter word.

V

vacant, vacuous   *Vacant* means *empty, without contents* (*house/post/seat that is vacant*) and can denote lack of thought, intelligence or awareness (*vacant smile*). *Vacuous* also means *empty* but is almost always used to mean *stupid, inane* in a much stronger way than *vacant* does (*vacuous explanation/expression/behaviour*). A person who gives you a *vacant* look may be quite intelligent but temporarily abstracted or puzzled; a person who gives a *vacuous* one is unintelligent.

valuable, valued

> *valuable*:   having great value (e.g. because of rarity, quality or usefulness) especially in monetary terms (*valuable information/necklace/advice*).
> *valued*:   highly regarded and esteemed (*valued helper, customer, friend*).

See **invaluable**.

valueless: see **invaluable**.

vantage, advantage   The first is an old-fashioned form of the second and is now seldom used except for the expression *vantage point*, a favourable position affording one an overall view.

vapid: see **tepid**.

vaunt: see **flaunt**.

venal, venial   Because of the well-known expression *venial sin* people assume that *venial* means *very wicked*. It means the opposite, in fact: *pardonable, not grave*. It is mortal sin that is unforgivable.

  Venal is *open to bribery, corrupt* and may be applied to individual people or to organisations (*a venal government*).

vengeance, revenge   These nouns correspond to the verbs **avenge, revenge** respectively. *Vengeance* implies just retribution. *Revenge* implies vindictiveness. Both mean *action to punish injury received*.

  The expression *with a vengeance* has nothing to do with *vengeance*. It means *in an extreme degree*.

venial: see **venal**.

venture, adventure   An undertaking that involves uncertainty, risk or danger may be called either an *adventure* or a *venture*. The former is more appropriate for surprising or exciting events, the latter for a speculative business undertaking.

  As verbs, both mean *take a risk*. *Adventure* is better when the risk is physical or involves danger or excitement. *Venture*, the more common verb, is preferable when the risk involves no more than inconvenience (*venture out of doors*), financial loss or opposition (*venture an opinion*). But in practice the words are often used interchangeably, which is quite acceptable.

verbal: see **aural**.

verbiage, verbosity   Both mean *the excessive use of words*. *Verbiage* is additionally often confusing or meaningless, *verbosity* pedantic or boring. Another distinction is that *verbiage* is usually written and *verbosity* spoken. One normally speaks of a person's *verbosity* and of the *verbiage* in a document.

verify, corroborate
  verify: ascertain the truth of.

vestige

> *corroborate*: confirm or support (especially by providing fresh evidence); make more certain.

There is an important difference here: a person who corroborates another's story may be corroborating a lie. A person who verifies a story proves it to be true.

vestige: see **trace** and **vestigial**.

vestigial, rudimentary Although synonymous in the technical and biological sense of (roughly) *imperfectly developed* these are distinct in everyday use.

> *vestigial*: showing only a small trace or hint of something vanished (*the vestigial remains of a Roman settlement*).
>
> *rudimentary*: basic, fundamental (*rudimentary exercises in grammar*).

For **vestige** see **trace**.

victory: see **win**.

vigorous, rigorous

> *vigorous*: full of vigour, force, energy, strength.
>
> *rigorous*: full of rigour, strictness, severity, accuracy.

There is some overlap – *vigorous measures*, for instance, are likely to be also *rigorous* if they are to succeed – but the two adjectives have distinct emphases.

Note how the associated nouns *vigour* and *rigour* differ from the adjectives in their spelling.

visit, visitation The longer word is more formal, less common, and restricted to a few special senses – an official visit, especially for inspection or examination; a special dispensation of divine reward or punishment; a severe trial or affliction (*a visitation of the plague*); the appearance of a supernatural being.

vocation, avocation The latter is sometimes improperly used for the former.

> *vocation*: profession, trade, employment.
>
> *avocation*: a diversion from one's employment, e.g. a subsidiary occupation, a hobby.

In other words an *avocation* is a distraction from a *vocation*.

voodoo: see **hoodoo**.

voracious: see **rapacious**.

W

wait, await *Wait* is intransitive, i.e. it does not take a direct object: we can say *Wait here* but not *Wait it*. *Await* is transitive and has to have a direct object or be in the passive. Hence *Why are we waiting* (not *awaiting*)?; *Wait until the bell rings* but *await the news/outcome/decision*. *Await* is uncommon, and rather formal except in a few standard phrases such as *A shock awaited him*. The usual transitive form is *wait for* (*Wait for it/the bus/the noise to stop*); the *for* is sometimes dropped, giving *wait* a transitive feel (*Wait your turn*).

waive, wave To *waive* is to refrain from demanding (one's right, etc.) or enforcing (one's claim, etc.). There can be no excuse for confusion with the many familiar senses of *wave* except in the expression *wave aside*, meaning *dismiss* (as with a gesture); this should never be *waive aside*.

wake: see **awake**.

waken: see **awake**.

wander, wonder
    wander: roam, stray, digress.
    wonder: feel surprise; desire to know; try to decide.
Wander rhymes with *fonder* and *wonder* with *blunder*.

warrant, warranty A *warranty* is a legal document, most commonly encountered as one given to a purchaser to guarantee the quality of goods and their repair or replacement if they are found to be defective, but the word also exists, with other meanings, in remoter branches of the law. A *warrant* is a document that gives authority for an action or decision: it may have legal force (*warrant for person's arrest*; *search-warrant*) or simply the weight of authority (*a travel warrant*).
    See also **guarantee**.

wary: see **chary**.

waste, wastage *Wastage* is not merely a showier alternative to *waste*, however much it may be used as such. Whereas *waste* is something squandered through carelessness or inefficiency, *wastage* is loss through legitimate use, such as wear, leakage or decay. *Waste* is deplorable, *wastage* simply inevitable.

wave

Natural wastage is often used to denote the reduction in size of a workforce by retirement or voluntary resignation as distinct from dismissal or other forced means.

wave: see **waive**.

way, weigh   *Weigh* is sometimes used instead of *way* in *under way* because of confusion with the expression *weigh anchor*. The fact that some dictionaries record *under weigh* means that it exists, not that it is right. It should be avoided.

wed, marry   *Marry* is the usual word. *Wed*, which means the same, has a respectable history in literature, but is now largely confined to journalism, which prefers short words in headlines, and to informal expressions such as *get wed* (i.e. marry). It is little used in everyday speech or writing.

Wedded to is more likely to mean *committed to* (*political party wedded to the past*) rather than *married to*.

weigh: see **way**.

wet, wetted; whet, whetted   The verb *wet* has the past tense and past participle *wet* or *wetted*. The second tends to be used of deliberate action (*He wetted the brickwork to make the plaster stick more readily*). Otherwise, *wet* is the more common form.

Whet, which has *whetted* as both past tense and past participle, means *sharpen* and, figuratively, *stimulate* as in *whet the appetite/one's curiosity*.

whatever, what ever   The traditional guidance has been that *what ever* should be used when an interrogative pronoun is needed and the *ever* is merely emphatic (*What ever will he do next?*), and that *whatever* is used in all other cases as a relative pronoun (*Take whatever you need*) or adjective (*No use whatever*). The rule holds good, but is not much followed. Most writers opt for *whatever* in all circumstances.

whenever, when ever   If *ever* is used to add emphasis to a question it should be written as a separate word (*When ever will we be able to afford it?*). When it carries a general sense of *no matter* it is written as part of a single word. In *Come whenever you wish*, *whenever* means *no matter when*.

This distinction, though well established, is increasingly ignored (and meaningless in speech, of course). The use of the single word in all circumstances is now common, though careful writers persist with the correct versions.

194

wherever, where ever The explanation and advice given under **whenever** hold good for *wherever* and *where ever*.
See also **whatever**.

whet: see **wet**.

while, whilst The primary sense of *while* is *during the time that* (as in *Nero fiddled while Rome burned*). It can also mean *although* or *whereas*, with the danger of ambiguity: *My wife sings while I play the tuba* is probably intended to mean *whereas I play* . . . but the primary sense of *during the time that* is strong and, as here, can produce an unintentionally comic effect. In the interests of clarity there is an argument that *whilst* should be used for *although/whereas* but in fact it means exactly the same as *while* in all senses, except that it is more old-fashioned and increasingly rare.

whisky, whiskey *Whisky* is made in Scotland and *whiskey* in Ireland and North America. In the USA both bourbon and Scotch are *whiskey*.

whither, wither The old-fashioned word for *to what place* or *to where* is *whither*. For *dry up*, *shrivel* and the figurative *abash* (*withering look*) *wither* is required. A horse's *withers* are between the shoulder bones.

whoever, who ever The usage explained under **whenever** and **whatever** applies also to *whoever* and *who ever*.

who's, whose *Who's* is the abbreviated form of *who is* or *who has*. *Whose* means *belonging to whom* or *of whom*.

win, victory *Win* as a noun meaning a *victory*, gain or success, especially in a sporting contest, is well established but still felt by some commentators to be slightly informal or journalistic. *Win* can certainly not be used as an alternative to *victory* when referring to success in a war, argument or conflict with adversity.

wince, flinch Dictionaries give both of these as meaning *shrink* or *draw back*, *start slightly* or *tense the muscles* – all of these involuntarily and as if from pain. In practice *flinch* is the word normally used to denote drawing back (*boxer flinched from the blow*) and it is the only possible choice in such figurative contexts as *never flinched from his responsibilities*. *Wince* is normally used of pulling a face in pain or as if in pain: figuratively it means *feel the pain of embarrassment* as in *a sense of humour that makes people wince*.

wit, humour   *Humour* is the general word for anything that gives rise to laughter or amusement. *Wit* is more specifically the branch of humour that lies in the clever perception of unexpected connections between disparate ideas in a way that is amusing or illuminating.

wither: see **whither**.

woebegone, woeful
> *woebegone*: looking sorrowful or miserable (*woebegone expression/appearance*).
> *woeful*: full of sorrow (*a woeful tale*); pitiful (*a woeful lack of tact*).

wonder: see **wander**.

won't, wont   *Won't* is the contraction of *will not*. *Wont* is an adjective meaning *accustomed* (*as he was wont to do*) or a noun meaning *habitual custom* (*as was his wont*); it is a shade old-fashioned, seldom used outside the expressions quoted. It is pronounced like *won't*.

woolly, woollen
> *woollen*: made of wool (*woollen socks*); for the manufacture of wool (*woollen mills*).

Woolly is a more informal word for *made of wool* (*woolly hat*) and can also mean *like wool, fluffy*. Figuratively it is a disparaging term for *tangled, unclear* (*woolly argument/thinking*) and also occurs in the expression *wild and woolly* meaning *boisterous*.

Both can be used as nouns for *something made of wool*.

worthless, priceless   Despite looking like synonyms, these are opposites:
> *worthless*: having no worth.
> *priceless*: having a worth beyond price.

worthwhile, worth while   Both mean *deserving time and effort*. *Worthwhile* is the adjectival form used before a noun: *a worthwhile visit*. It is still customary to use *worth while* after a verb (*The visit was worth while*) just as one would use the separate words in *The visit was worth my while* where *worth* means *meriting* and *while* is a noun meaning *time and trouble spent*.

The distinction is, however, on the wane, and *The visit was worthwhile* would not now cause any raised eyebrows.

wrack: see **rack**.

wrapped: see **rapt**.

wrath, wroth Easily confused by virtue of being uncommon.
    wrath (noun):   anger (Rhymes with *moth*).
    wroth (adjective):   angry (Rhymes with *both*).
    Before a noun the usual word is *wrathful. Wroth* is now archaic.

wreak: see **reap**.

wreaked: see **wrought**.

wroth: see **wrath**.

wrought, wreaked *Wrought* is the archaic past tense or past participle
of *work* but is most likely to be encountered as an adjective meaning
worked into shape by artistry (carefully wrought) or *deeply stirred* as in
overwrought or *wrought-up.*
    Wreaked is the past form of *wreak* meaning *inflict (wreaked
havoc/vengeance)* or *give free rein to (wreaked her anger on him).*

Y

yoke, yolk *Yolk* is generally confined to eggs. For all other senses the
spelling *yoke* is needed.

young, youthful *Young* is factual, and can be applied to things and
animals as well as people (*young country; in his young days*). *Youthful* is
normally restricted to people and implies the attractive qualities of
youth such as freshness and vitality (*man of youthful appearance*).

Z

zany, zombie A *zombie* is, in witchcraft, either a spirit that is said to
bring a corpse to life or a corpse thus reanimated. A person described
as a *zombie* is thus like a walking corpse, without animation or
judgement. A *zany*, however, is a clown or buffoon: as an adjective
zany means *comical in a crazy or fantastical way.*

zeal, zest

     zeal: keen, sometimes fanatical, interest in pursuit of something, especially a cause or ideal.

     zest: keen enjoyment (*zest for life*); flavour, added interest (*bring zest to the proceedings*).

zombie: see **zany**.